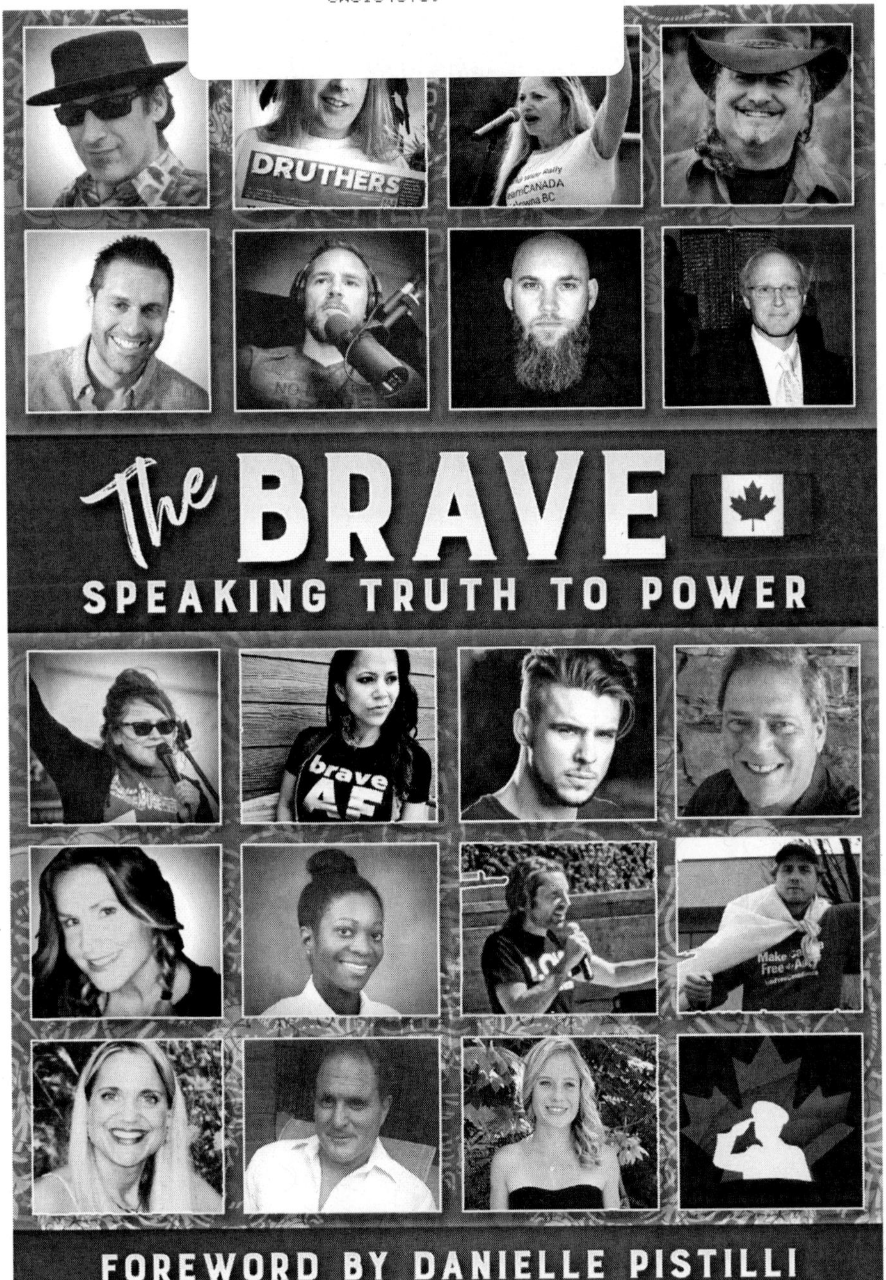
DRUTHERS
The BRAVE
SPEAKING TRUTH TO POWER
brave AF
FOREWORD BY DANIELLE PISTILLI

The Brave: Speaking Truth to Power

ISBN: 978-1-7775400-2-9

DISCLAIMER: This book is for entertainment and education purposes only. It is not intended to serve as business advice. This book is not intended to instruct or advise in any way. Using any of the information in this book is based on the reader's own judgment after consulting with his or her trusted professionals. The views expressed herein are not necessarily those of the publisher, nor the other co-authors. The resources provided in this book are based upon the recommendations of each individual author and may change or cease to exist without notice. Further, the systems, techniques, and suggestions presented here may have been successful for the co-author, but the reader may not receive the same results or any results at all. All company names and product names are copyrights of the respective owners. None of the owners of products or services mentioned herein have endorsed this publication; they are simply mentioned as examples of resources that the reader might find helpful. While all attempts have been made to verify the information provided herein, the publisher assumes no responsibility for errors, omissions, or misunderstandings on the subject matter. The reader assumes full responsibility for their own actions with regards to their use of this information. No guarantees are made.

Lionheart Publishing
Website: www.LadyBravenofthePride.com
E-mail: lanigelera@hotmail.com
Instagram: @LadyBravenofthePride

Dedicated to

The Brave

This book is dedicated to all those who stood up, spoke out, and refused to be told to sit back down; for all of those who proclaimed their truth in the face of evil, corruption, and fraud; for every single man and woman that was told that their voice didn't matter and that they alone could not make a difference in the battle for our lives; and for every Canadian that has lost a loved one, their career, job, and income to mind control and brainwashing because they refused to be coerced into injecting themselves with poison.

Many of us have lost a great deal because we chose to speak truth to power. We chose to defend our children and loved ones that were being programmed and manipulated. We chose to hold corrupt public officials accountable for their crimes against humanity. We chose to fight for what is right, for what is just, and for the freedom we value in this great country of ours.

By sharing your brave stories of speaking truth to power at this time of great awakening, you will inspire and empower a nation to courageously take back our sovereign health and rights from a communist dictatorship. Your righteous actions and your valid voices are being heard and are making bigger waves around the country than you will ever know.

Thank you for following your heart, defending our Canadian Charter of Rights and Freedoms, and for working toward the future we all want and envision with Peace, Unity, Prosperity, and Love for all!

Table of Contents

Foreword – Danielle Pistilli 1

1. LANI GELERA – Unite the Lions 6

2. DARLENE ONDI – The Phoenix Rising 18

3. MATT BELAIR – The Sin of Silence 32

4. DAVID WHITEHEAD – Truth Warrior 41

5. OWEN OWEN OWEN – The Great Social Experiment 51

6. DAVID LINDSAY – What can I do? 69

7. JASON CHRISTOFF – Truth to Power 82

8. ALEX LASAREV – Love is My New Normal 94

9. TED KUNTZ – My Journey to Truth and Power 100

10. MARCELLA DESJARLAIS – How They Remember You 113

11. DANNA BRESCIANI – The Liberti Club 120

12. POLICE ON GUARD FOR THEE – Breaking Ranks 129

13. SHAWN JASON – Throwing a Wrench in The Machine 141

14. MITCH MURPHY – Red Pill Rapper 150

15. DAVID PILZ – Every Word Matters 160

16. NORDIA GERMAN – Truth, Freedom, and Health 174

17. CALLIE OCEAN – Standing in Truth at 17 182

18. DR. STEPHEN MALTHOUSE – The Doctors 192

19. KRISTAL NICOLE PITTER – Voice of Truth 203

20. RC THE RAPPER – The Logical Choice 216

Thank You to the Brave Donors! 245

About Lionheart Publishing 246

Foreword

Danielle Pistilli

In a world full of lies, deceit, corruption, and deception, finding truth these days is like finding a needle in a haystack. One of the greatest attributes one may possess in life may very well be the ability to have discernment.

There are always going to be different versions of the truth. Your truth, someone else's truth, and then, of course, the real truth. The question is: How do you decide what the real truth is? How do you take what you have learned and pass that knowledge on, without regurgitating a possible false truth or adding to the misinformation highway?

Of course, one does not have to dig very deep to find corruption in the food or medical industries, nor need a Harvard degree to figure out that not all "$cience" is truth, but more and more it is becoming blatantly obvious that social media and the mainstream media talking-heads are censoring truth and regurgitating everything they are told to say, all for the sake of protecting these industries and the governments that are in bed with them. With social media and the mainstream media lying and censoring real truth, in the name of control and the almighty dollar, we need to work twice as hard to cut through the darkness to see the light.

It's no wonder so many people stay in cognitive dissonance about all of the corruption. The thought of someone spending years in school or in a particular career, only to find out they have been unknowingly propagating an industry filled with untruths, is way too much for some to handle. Burying their heads in the sand, avoiding the truth, and arguing what they know to be true are often a person's only defense mechanisms to avoid looking like their education and career choices were not a total waste of time and money. It's disturbing how many people mistake education for intelligence these days. It baffles me, really, how many "smart people" there are in this world that lack serious intelligence when it comes to this Great Awakening when there are signs everywhere! This leaves me thinking there are very few people that I would consider taking into battle with me, because of their inability to discern real truth. A big shout out to those that recognized that they were in one of the mentioned industries and are speaking out about it and are making a difference in their corner of the world, to make things right! We know it hasn't been easy.

World War III (aka the COVID deception) has been called a spiritual war and an information or psychological battle by many. Those that don't understand the grand totality of what is going on often ask questions like: "Why would our government do this to us?" or "Why would every country be involved with this?". It's understandably difficult to comprehend that so many people could possibly be involved in the deception, until you understand who is really at the root of this evil plan. It has been said that the biggest lie the world ever knew was believing that the devil didn't exist. If anyone wants to find the answers to these gloomy questions, they had better start opening their eyes to the reality that he, or it, plays a bigger role in this mess than most people would care to admit. If people think that their government cares for them and has their best interests at heart, then none of this fiasco will ever make sense, but if you consider, for a moment, that the devil has been working on this plan to destroy everything good on this planet since the beginning of time, and that those in power use the devil's arsenal of bribery, coercion, and manipulation to run the world, then it ALL makes sense!

Think about it: all the wars created under invisible terrorism or an "invisible enemy"; the education system, which was only created to teach one theory of thinking to gain mass control over a young society; chemtrails and GMOs to poison our environment; global warming to scare people into believing there are too many of us on the planet; vaccinations for your children or they are told they may die or spread disease; limited treatment options like chemotherapy and radiation for cancers; BLM and other race and gender divisional tactics that create the very divide they say they are trying to eliminate; organizations that are meant to protect children but are really harming them and have been used for trafficking; and the fear that has been perpetuated by the media since the beginning of this *plandemic*, which is, of course, the biggest lie ever, known as COVID-19. All deception! All lies! All day! Every day! It's damn near impossible to escape. But for those of us willing to look at the truth, we can actually begin to make changes.

History is truly hard to define when so much of what we have been taught has been twisted, but there are hints everywhere if we have eyes to see and ears to hear. From the first language of Hebrew came Latin. If you haven't already looked up the Latin word for "pharmacy", I suggest checking it out. It translates to *pharmacia*, which means a preparer of drug, poison, or spell, or witchery and sorcery. And as if that wasn't enough of a sign, the symbol that represents the entire industry is a snake, or serpent. Biblically speaking, the serpent was a symbol of evil power and chaos from the underworld. Make no mistake, this industry is not stupid. These words and symbols are not chosen by accident or coincidence. It's time to rip off the rose-coloured glasses and stop thinking that the Rockefeller/Rothchild funded education systems were put here to save and protect us, because it is quite the opposite.

There is no room for cognitive dissonance at any level in this game. There is deception and coercion everywhere we look. Most who are reading this book would probably consider themselves to be “awake” to the corruption, and yet many take their lead from false idols that cause conflict and chaos everywhere they go. Do not be a sheep 2.0! I’m not looking to cast any insults here, but most of the sleepers think Bonnie Henry and Theresa Tam are nice too, but you wouldn’t catch anyone from the Freedom Movement dancing with those devils. One can be kind or a powerful leader and communicator and still not be truthful.

I don’t want to seem jaded, because before CV-19 hit, I was one of the most openly trusting, wanna-see-the-good-in-everyone gals, but I have come to realize that there are wolves in sheep’s clothing at every level. Just remember, Lucifer was one of the most beautiful angels before he fell, and deception can look integral, beautiful, and polite. Keep this in mind when discerning to whom you look for truth. Empty vessels speak the loudest. Those that scream things like “racist” are often the ones creating the division. Watch who surrounds themselves in mayhem and chaos, even if the action or movement looks like it's for a wonderful, well-meaning, inspiring cause, as there may be a bigger plan in motion to derail us down the road. And don’t forget, finding the truth always becomes easier when you just follow the money.

There are good people battling this war, and thanks to the producer of this book, Lani Gelera, she is bringing light to many of their inspirational stories, *Speaking Truth to Power*. Guard this book with your life. Censorship on social media is the new book-burning, and who knows if history will repeat itself again with the real books. Every writer in this *Brave* series plays a role in revealing and exposing truth. Many of them never saw themselves rising up as activists, or fighting for humanity or for our children, but they have all stepped up in some way, shape, or form. They were all called to make change. Called to stand in the fire of ridicule, lost relationships, and lost jobs. Called to be brave. And thank God they are! Without "The Brave" standing up and speaking out, our world wouldn't have a chance. Take as much as you can from their stories and implement them in your own life and in your community.

Thank you, Lani, for giving us the opportunity to speak our truth, and thank you to those that have inspired me to inspire others. This is what these chapters and this series of books is all about. It represents a piece of history -- our history. Let it inspire and empower you to take action and to make the change you wish to see in the world.

To Our Freedom!

Dani

Chapter One

Unite the Lions

By Lani Gelera

The Brave: Courage During COVID, published in May 2021, was a big success across the country in the fight for our freedom movement. From concept, compilation, editing, formatting, and publishing, only three months had passed. I was a busy girl, learning as I went along, making mistakes, refocusing, and pushing through the project, while the entire time I felt I was being guided and protected by spirit.

The first volume of *The Brave* was well-received as an inspiration to take courageous action, encouragement to believe in a better future, and an empowering wealth of counternarrative true conscious information. There is a small percentage of the Canadian population that is drawn to the truth like a moth to flame. They have become truth seekers out of necessity as they could see through the veil of deception, mind control, and programming propagated by the mainstream media.

The stories of fellow freedom fighters, truth-seekers, and justice activists from all across the country who are standing up to government corruption and medical fraud, courageously in the face of tyranny and oppression, will become a part of our true Canadian history and heritage. *The Brave* book series has been envisioned as a factual reference for what has really taken place during the great awakening of humanity.

After reading and fully comprehending all of the brave stories that I compiled in the first book, I was activated and compelled to take courageous aligned action myself! I decided that if all of these brave freedom fighters across the country could organize and hold freedom rallies in their hometowns to share alternative news and true conscious information, then so could I. Many of the stories were from every day, relatable, good-hearted Canadians that were just doing what they could to make a difference, even in the face of unlawful COVID restrictions, rules, mandates, provincial orders, costly fines, and the threat of losing their friends, families, and livelihoods.

Because they were brave, because they were bold, because they stood up for themselves, their beliefs, their loved ones, their freedom, and their futures, I was inspired to do the same. How's that for a personal testimony about the first book in The Brave series?

Sea To Sky Freedom Protestival

At the end of April, I began organizing and manifesting the Sea to Sky Freedom Protestival to be held in my hometown of Squamish on May 22. A friend of mine had used the word "Protestival" and I thought that it adequately described the kind of event I wanted to plan with a festival feeling of fun and community while standing up and protesting unlawful human rights violations and government corruption.

This was extremely challenging for me because I have never organized a big event like this, and although there were a few dozen local freedom thinkers that said they supported me, there was no one else in this sleepy little mountain tourist town that was willing to bravely stand up beside me and help me put the event together. I was on my own. Fortunately, I had started building a strong connection with my brave freedom family. When I felt drained and down, tired and defeated, or started questioning myself, they were always there to pick me backup and set me on track again.

The true colours of the local long-time residents came out and they lashed out at me publicly with fear mongering, hatred, and obvious self-loathing. They declared me the "enemy of Squamish" for even suggesting counter-narrative information they felt would put them all at risk for catching the virus by organizing a peaceful event in a park in downtown Squamish. These are the same people who promoted gaslighting and shaming of people to wear their muzzles to save lives and to take your vaxx and be a responsible member of society. They do not know what they do. "Forgive them" was a constant mantra in my mind as they viciously attacked me psychically, energetically, verbally, and at every opportunity I gave them online.

It's a good thing that I don't have a reputation or an ego that I felt the need to defend or protect, because they had their way with me in the local papers, too. I didn't engage in their hateful rhetoric and low vibration. I saw little benefit to fanning their flames with any response at all and I chose to ignore them while I was focusing on my mission at hand. I was determined to hold a peaceful, fun, empowering, alternative community-building event for all of those who have no access to the truth because of the pervasive mainstream media mind-control programming all over the news, radio, and municipal community communications.

There were plenty of Squamish residents that were questioning the narrative, but because of the low vibe fear-mongering, hate speech, and threats of boycotting any person or business that questioned the CV narrative, they were afraid to stand up, speak out, or even be seen as a CV denier, anti-masker, or conspiracy theorist. Those are the people to whom I wanted to reach out. Those are the Sea to Sky residents for whom I wanted to hold this event. I had decided that I was going to bring all those who questioned the fake news, and I was going to teach them how to be brave. This is what I call "Uniting the Lions".

The Sea to Sky Freedom Protestival was held on a beautiful sunny day in May. All the events were carried out peacefully and with the highest vibrations of love, laughter, singing, dancing, and counter-narrative informational empowerment for the entire conscious community in the Sea to Sky corridor. Everything went smoothly, as planned, from the Pemberton and Vancouver car rallies to the event, to the Freedom March around downtown Squamish. There were bouncy castles, bubbles, face painting, and fun for the children to play while the adults danced and sang with like-minded brave lions and shared important relevant information that could save lives but has been censored and kept from us by the mainstream media mafia. The entire event was a success because I planned it that way.

A few days after the event, I noticed that our very own mayor, Karen Elliot, had some nasty things to say about the event on a public Facebook forum. I don't normally respond to the horrible haters and those propagating the lies and living in fear, but I thought this was a good opportunity to speak truth to power and call Karen out on her lack of support for the truth, or for those of us in the community that were not falling for her false narrative and fear-porn propaganda.

So, I wrote a very public "Dear Karen" letter. I posted it all over my Facebook and I tagged her in it. Also, I sent a copy to the local The Chief newspaper, which they did not post.

The letter read as follows:

May 26, 2021

To Karen Elliot,

Mayor, District of Squamish, BC

Dear Karen,

I would like to respond to your public comment on Facebook regarding the Sea to Sky Freedom Protestival that I organized last weekend. You said, “It wasn’t approved. It was an illegal event given the health orders. Police will issue fines. People do have a constitutional right to do this. It is disgusting and horrible, I agree.”

I would like to take this opportunity to correct you and inform you about the event that you missed. We do not need your approval or permission to protest the actions of our government with which we do not agree. We do not need your approval or permission to peacefully unite for the purpose of sharing true conscious counter-narrative information that has been censored and kept from the public.

The event was not illegal. We did not break a single law. The RCMP were informed about the event a month ahead of time and I was in contact with them about potential concerns and problems. I politely and respectfully requested that they attend to keep the peace and guide traffic. That is their job. They did attend and they did help keep the peace and guide traffic during the protest march. They did not hand out any fines to anyone because no one broke the law.

There is an exceptionally large contingent of Squamish residents that are questioning the fear-mongering and control narrative that you are propagating. There were between 150-200 peaceful protesters that attended the rally, but there are hundreds, if not thousands, more that support the freedom movement. The reason they did not attend in person is because of the public persecution, boycotting, and bullying of those who believe all the lies from the mainstream media and believe they can coerce, condemn, and gaslight others into submission and silence.

I am going to stand up and speak out for everyone that is afraid of the backlash and bullies. We have freedom of speech, and I am not afraid to use my voice.

There was nothing disgusting or horrible about the event. It was an extremely peaceful, high vibrational, inspiring, empowering, and encouraging event advocating for freedom of speech, freedom of choice, freedom from censorship, freedom to travel, and freedom from control by a corrupt government that does not have the best interests of the people in mind.

The event was amazing because I organized and planned it that way. It would have been nice if you were there. You may have been inspired. Are you open to having a counter-narrative conversation about the concerns of Squamish residents and business owners that do not believe all they have been told by the false mainstream media's fear-mongering propaganda? I would love to open the conversation.

Sincerely,

Lani Gelera
Squamish Resident

I honestly believe that this letter was so well written, to the point, clear, concise, and kind, with the invitation to have a counter-narrative conversation, that there is no way that Karen could have responded without exposing her own corruption in going along with a false narrative and government tyranny. There really isn't much she could have said. So she didn't say a single word. Instead, two weeks after the rally, I received a phone call from the local RCMP sergeant with whom I was in connection and collaboration to hold the event. He informed me that he had a ticket fine for $2300 for me for holding an illegal unauthorized event. He asked where I was, then he then came to where I was having my brunch with a friend and gave me the ticket in person. I video recorded the interaction for my own notes, but I shared it online to let others know that it was just a fine, I was going to deal with it, and that I couldn't be coerced or threatened in this way. I felt as though he believed he was just doing his job. But his job was not to follow orders from a corrupt politician. His job was to uphold the Charter rights and our right to protest the actions of our government, to which he swore an oath. He was going along with tyranny and not performing his duties as a public servant.

Most people would have panicked or been upset about receiving a ticket for $2,300, but not me. I saw this as the most amazing divine opportunity to handle this situation differently and show the people what it truly means to speak truth to power. Everything was happening for a reason, and I could see the path to victory before me -- not by fighting this fine in a legal court, but by beginning my spiritual journey to take back my power as a woman and learn about the original and true Law of Man.

The concept of Equity was first introduced to me by one of the authors of my first book. And as everything is divine in perfect timing, I was drawn to her and her partner to learn as much as I could about becoming a private citizen and attaining my birthright sovereignty. This is not something you can learn overnight or take a single course to master. You are essentially re-learning how to speak, how to look at everything in a different way, how to take back your power, how to remove controversy from your life, and how to make a claim and attain your birthright abundance. You have to be willing to accept that the words we use have many meanings and we have been using them to our disadvantage our whole lives. Almost everything we have ever learned about the nature of our reality is a lie, and the lie was designed to keep us in a system of slavery and prevent us from ever knowing how truly powerful we are.

Since I began this quest for knowledge, four other unrelated parties have come into my social sphere of influence to start sharing their individual perspective and approach to gain this kind of wisdom. Most of them have been studying Equity Law, God's Law, Natural Law, or the Law of Man for over 30-40 years and I find it divine providence that they are all converging in my awareness on the same timeline and frequency as I am at this point in our lives. Everything is divine and everything is on time.

If you would like to learn more about how I am proceeding to address my ticket, you will have to stay tuned for future updates in the next volume of *The Brave*. If you would like to learn more about the law of man knowledge, I would have to say that obtaining this information is very much a spiritual journey, and if you are ready to expand your mind and awareness, the opportunity to research and study Divine Law will present itself to you in the higher dimensions of consciousness. If you are not sure what that means, maybe you are not quite ready.

I will definitely be sharing more stories and writing more about these relevant higher vibrational, higher consciousness concepts of God's Law, Spiritual Law, Karmic Law, and the Law of Man in my next Brave book in the series, volume 3, called, The Brave: Ascending Human Consciousness.

Communicating with Compassion

One thing I have learned by standing in my power and speaking truth to the masses and to the powers that be is that not everyone can hear me. Sometimes I feel like I am screaming from the top of the mountain and only a very few within a certain distance can even hear my voice in the wind. Only those that are also climbing the mountain or almost at the top can comprehend the words I speak. Everyone else is oblivious to what I am saying because they are not close enough to hear.

Since March 2020, I have been saying that this entire fake pandemic was leading up to a nefarious vaccine and the evil powers that be were trying to depopulate the planet. It was plain as day to see since they had advertised their UN Agenda 21, Lock-Step, Georgia Guidestones, Denver Airport, and many more plans to commit genocide. Those that thought I was crazy back at the beginning of the pandemic are just starting to see the hidden agenda now in August 2021. But they couldn't hear me back then and I have spent over a year trying to figure out the best way to communicate with compassion in a way that those I love and care for can hear my plea to question the narrative they have embraced and defend. Our *Crime Minister* Trudeau and our demonic British Columbia government have just announced their intention to implement the vaccine passport.

Speaking Truth to Power

The entire purpose of compiling all of these inspiring stories in this volume of The Brave was to help activate our own individual throat chakras and empower us all to start standing up and speaking out against those who wish to enslave all of mankind in a system of oppression and tyrannical communism. I know for a fact that I was not born on this planet at this time in the history of humanity to sit down, stay quiet, do as I'm told, obey, and comply with tyranny while those I love are dying and most everyone else is falling victim to brainwashing and mind control.

By sharing true conscious stories of other brave freedom fighters across the country speaking out and making a difference in their communities, I sincerely hope to ignite the soul fire within and mobilize all those who have thought even for one second that their voice didn't matter or that they had no power to effect change in the world.

I want to remind everyone that true change in the world, in our world or any world, always begins by changing ourselves from within. By changing our perspective, by healing our mortal wounds, and by expanding our awareness and consciousness we all have the power to effect massive change for all of humanity. But we must start our journey from within. Open eyes, open mind, open heart, open arms.

We are so much stronger, braver, wiser, more capable, and more powerful than any authority figure has ever allowed us to believe about ourselves. The struggles in the past year have reminded me of my true power, my God-given unalienable rights, and my inherent divine nature. I've learned a lot about what my true values are and what I am willing to sacrifice, to walk away from, or to die for in this spiritual and psychological war. I took some of Yoda's advice and trained myself to let go of all I feared to lose. I had to decide for myself what my purpose was here on earth and what hill I was willing to die on.

"Freedom's just another word for nothing left to lose
Nothing don't mean nothing, honey, if it ain't free"
~ Janis Joplin

Now is the time to come together with resonant souls and speak our truth.

Now is the time to demand that those people in positions of power are held accountable for their evil and satanic crimes against humanity.

Now is the time to support, encourage, empower, and love each other as we navigate our way through the storm that has only just begun.

Now is the time to take back our divine power and take back our country!

Now is the time to Unite The Lions!

About Lani - Lady Braven of the Pride

LANI survived a childhood of emotional trauma and adversity. She then grew up to be an independent, confident, and courageous Professional Stunt-woman in Hollywood North TV and Film. After falling down for a living for 20 years, the concepts of overcoming and facing fear, developing authentic self-love and self-respect with integrity, and standing up for her beliefs and values were forged into every fiber of her being. Her connection to spirit has reminded her how divine and powerful she truly was, and she aims to share that remembrance with the rest of the world.

Lani is a Courage Coach, an Energy Healer, a Light Worker, and CEO of Lionheart Publishing. She is a Best-Selling Author and has been writing for adventure magazines, blogs, and articles for the past 6 years. Assisting humanity in elevating our collective consciousness and vibration with courage and compassion is, without a shadow of a doubt, exactly what she is meant to be doing at this point during the Great Awakening of Humanity.

Lani is a good woman with the best intentions and clean hands. Since Lani is passionate about bringing like-minded brave lions together, she has assigned herself a new title as Lady Braven of the Pride. And so it is.

Follow Lani on Instagram @LadyBravenofthePride

or website: www.ladybravenofthepride.com

Chapter Two

<u>The Phoenix Rising</u>

By Darlene Ondi

Destiny or Fate?

Haven't we all heard the words "How did I get here?"

It is with this thought in mind that I start my story.

It is April 2021. I never thought I would be alive at this time. Literally! My journey has been fraught with depression, anxiety/agoraphobia, severe panic attacks, BDD (body dysmorphic disorder), and numerous failed suicide attempts. I realized at the age of 30 that I was meant to be here and so began the first steps of my healing towards self-love.

I've always appreciated the unusual, so I would go for readings. If I would have actually believed that a psychic whom I had seen decades ago was correct when she made the audacious statement that she saw me somehow involved in politics, I would have rolled on the floor laughing hysterically. Seriously! If I've said it once I've said it a thousand times: GOD certainly has a wickedly wild sense of humour! So, I find myself, right here and right now, living my most recent chapter as a full-blown Freedom Fighter and Truth Seeker/Activist.

My name is Darlene. I have now been on this planet for five and a half decades. Life is not one iota close to what I thought it would be. Because of my personal experiences, I have a clearer understanding of terms such as "follow your bliss", "blossom where you land", and "when someone shows you who they are the first time, believe them". I've met liars, cheats, betrayers, tyrants, and, as the pendulum swings, conscious, exceptional, and gorgeous on the inside and out humans along this journey.

I was recently approached by my wonderful friend and fellow connector extraordinaire, Danielle Pistilli, to speak with a beautiful soul by the name of Lani Gelera. She was creating a series on "the Freedom Movement" and the courageous leaders making a stand. Lani felt these people would be a pinnacle part of Canadian History. Her second Brave project focused on Speaking Truth to Power. When I was asked, I knew this series was in alignment with me.

The theme of power and speaking to truth is exactly what I have been living and breathing this last year. I had, by this time, smelled the reek of filthy deception of the *plandemic*. And I yelled "Hell, NO!!!" when it came to taking my rights and freedoms away. There are massively tragic moments in your life where you remember exactly where you were and who you were with, and March of 2020 was one of those defining moments. I was already awake, but this agenda of "lockstep" opened me up to an entirely new level of courage and of finding my voice.

I came to realize that my traumatic life experiences had honed and prepared me for this very time. I'd already experienced tyranny, isolation, shaming, ridicule, harsh criticism, starvation, and physical punishment. I don't wish my experiences on anyone. However, those experiences have allowed me to respond from a more certain and powerful perspective. I sense that my previous metamorphosis of coming through the chrysalis prepared me to deal with situations with a strength that many are not able to comprehend.

The Joy of Giving

One of my biggest lessons in life is the difference between being in servitude to others and being in service to others. I was the child who was quiet, and I sought out those who were under-served, the "outcasts" of society, those who were vulnerable. I sense it is the foundation of why I became a social worker (Child Protection Worker). I wanted to help children because inwardly I knew that by revisiting some of my childhood trauma I would heal myself, and, in so doing, heal others. I was ultra-sensitive and an empath. I feel the emotions of others on a deep level. I wanted the people I served to know that I truly cared and that I carried great compassion and humility for their way of being. My goal was to make a difference in the life of at least one child. I sense I did that. Perhaps one day I will share more about my journey in this profession, which I eventually left because "the system" would not allow me to do the work that was necessary. When my joy left the work that I felt I had been called to do, I was again catapulted into the abyss of the unknown. I left my career, my province, my toxic relationship, and my friends, and I headed to Alberta. It was one of the many reminders of why truth and freedom were so important to me.

Create Your Mantras To Live By

There are several mantras I live by, and as an observer of people I have a deep resonance with "beautiful people don't just happen". Through my own trials and tribulations I have come to know that my greatest joy comes in service to others and in assisting them to strive towards their ever-evolving, highest, most magnificent sense of themselves. I know that we must have contrast in our lives to have that deeper understanding. One of mine was going from being completely disempowered to being empowered. I've felt great loss, which allowed me to exult in joy. I unintentionally created my own personal prison in relationships and work that taught myself that freedom is worth fighting for.

"Know Thyself" is one of my hardest yet most liberating mantras. I know that I cannot see something in someone that I do not hold within myself. Being judgmental was a big one for me, and I did a lot of self-talk, asking myself many times, "Who are *you* to judge, Darlene?" I never thought I had a controlling nature until I realized that I am not in control.

I was hyper critical of myself, and I had to learn the hard way that life is not fair, that life is precious, and to enjoy each and every moment of life. I have a choice: I can be bitter or get better. I chose to get better because I came to realize that I had no idea as to who I was. I had allowed others to tell me who to be, what to say, when to show up, when to leave, how much I was worth -- the list was endless. Now the government and health care system was telling me the same and I would have no part of it!

I learned to be kind to myself. I had to learn to forgive myself, and, once I did, I catapulted my road to healing. I started to release my old self -- the timid, shy, people-pleasing, low self-worth, hyper-critical, pathetic, angry, self-loathing, scared woman. I had to let go of my worries. My God, I worried about everything. In the past, I had the most horrendous panic attacks because of it. The pain was horrific. I thought sometimes I was going to die! When I share this today with people that I assist through my many Zooms and gatherings, they are awestruck. It is one of the main reasons I "practice what I preach" and teach what I do because I continue to see my own transformation. I know that if I can do it, anyone can!

Your WORD is your BOND, especially to yourself

Where has this chapter of life led me? To three of the most challenging and most fulfilling missions in my life:

1. Self-Love

2. Letting Go

3. Acceptance

I pray often.

I learned to BE and to BE QUIET.

I learned to BE grateful. Grateful to wake up every morning. Grateful for the air I breathe. Grateful for my body, which I once hated. Grateful for all my senses. Grateful to learn something new every day with the intention of making a difference each day in someone's life. Grateful for my community of peeps.

I decided to stand out and BE Seen.

Last March, my good friend, Susann Czekus, asked me to attend a Stuart Park rally in Kelowna, which led us to another rally in Vernon, BC. It was here that I heard Ted Kuntz speak. He is the president of Vaccine Choice Canada. This powerful organization is suing various elected and appointed officials over violations of our rights and freedoms with their COVID-19 restrictions. Part of his presentation was a video of a recent press conference he held where he was talking about that lawsuit with Rocco Galati, the top Canadian Constitutional lawyer representing the case.

The list of defendants is a short Who's Who of political and medical power brokers in

Canada and in the province of Ontario. This lawsuit was just the beginning. There have been many more lawsuits over the harm caused to the citizens of Canada through the irresponsible and unconstitutional use of emergency powers to shut down small businesses, put people out of work, shut down schools, limit access to health care, force mask-wearing and social distancing, and threaten us with taking away our rights to associate, travel, and make our own informed health decisions. All without any scientific facts to back up these draconian measures!

LIST OF DEFENDANTS IN THE JULY 2020 STATEMENT OF CLAIM:

Justin TRUDEAU, Prime Minister of Canada;

Dr. Theresa TAM, Chief Medical Officer for Canada;

Marc GARNEAU, Canadian Transport Minister;

Doug FORD, Premier of Ontario;

Christine ELLIOT, Minister of Health for Ontario;

Stephen LECCE, Minister of Education for Ontario;

Dr. David WILLIAMS, Ontario Chief Medical Officer;

CITY OF TORONTO;

John TORY, Mayor City of Toronto;

Dr. Eileen DE VILLA, Toronto Chief Medical Officer;

The County of WELLINGTON-DUFFERIN-GUELPH ("CWDG");

Nicola MERCER (Chief) Medical Officer for CWDG;

WINDSOR-ESSEX COUNTY;

Dr. Wajid AHMED (Chief) Medical Officer for Windsor-Essex County;

Her Majesty the Queen in Right of Canada;

Her Majesty the Queen in Right of Ontario;

Attorney General of Canada;

Attorney General of Ontario;

The Canadian Broadcasting Corporation ("CBC");

Johns and Janes DOE officials and employees of the above-noted defendants.

The majority of Canadians are clueless about the most important court case in Canadian history because the mainstream media has hidden it! This has to change!

Further into Ted's presentation, I learned that Ted's son, Joshua, had been murdered by the DPT vaccine (diphtheria pertussis tetanus). I couldn't stop bawling. I HAD TO DO SOMETHING! Thank you, Ted, for leading me back to my purpose of helping children.

On our drive back to Kelowna, three other ladies and I made the decision to host an event of our own. That led to The Grand Solution event at Bertram Regional Park, where we made history that day by "defying" the BC public health orders that no more than 50 people were to gather. Over 200 Freedom Fighters and Truth Seekers met, including families with their children, to show the government and other public servants who believed they had authority over us that WE DO NOT COMPLY! WE THE PEOPLE have rights and freedoms! What is stated in the Constitution of Canada is the "Supreme Law of Canada, and any law that is inconsistent with the provisions of the Constitution is, to the extent of its inconsistency, of no force or effect."

The rallies continued every Saturday, and I found myself becoming more and more involved in the Freedom Movement. Currently, I host calls for a grassroots movement called Action4Canada with co-founders Tanya Gaw and Mac Rogerson. Action4Canada has several campaigns, including getting masks off kids, opening businesses, opening churches, and numerous resources to assist others in filing complaints and understanding their rights and freedoms.

With my growing faith, courage, and confidence, I decided to host a couple of Zooms of my own because I was observing the necessity of people wanting to learn how to stand in their truth and courage. I host Zooms to educate on common law and conduct role plays of real-life situations, how to be prepared, and what to say. Tuesday mornings we meet in the community to go through topics that are top of mind. Consistency and practice are key if we are to prepare ourselves for the totalitarian tiptoe toward a second holocaust.

I currently scout for my great friend, Kynthea, who is the producer of *The Other Side of the News* with a listenership in over 160 countries. I've been given this platform to share what is happening in Canada with the world and I continue to have the honour and pleasure to connect with brilliant people such as Dr. Judy Mikovitz, who is a lifelong researcher and scientist. Dr. Judy has a PhD in Biochemistry and Molecular Biology. She has 40 years of experience in drug development and mechanisms of disease development.

Dr. Judy is a NY Times Best Seller and author of three books: *Plague*; *Plague of Corruption*; and *Case Against Masks*. Her testimonial on the movie, *Plandemic*, foreshadowed the level of corruption we Canadians are experiencing today.

Dr. Sherri Tenpenny is an Osteopathic Medical Doctor and has been in the practice of medicine since 1985. A four-day National Information Vaccine meeting in Washington, DC, in September of 2000, caused her to question. Dr. Tenpenny started by reading the 1998 CDC documents. That was 20 years ago and well over 40,000 hours of research and writing. She calls herself the "Go-To Girl" on problems dealing with vaccines and is one of the most widely heard doctors in the world.

Sterling Hill is a mother, confidante, and genetic genius. Amongst her many other roles, Sterling is also the founder of MTHFR (methylenetetrahydrofolate reductase) Support. She was awarded commendations by the Louisiana Senate for her commitment in defending the constitutional rights of citizens to make their own fully-informed medical decisions and her various defenses of the health of American children. Sterling works tirelessly to inform and educate the world against the genocide of which we find ourselves a part.

Gareth Icke is a musician, author, actor, and TV presenter. He is the son of the influential world-renowned public speaker and activist, David Icke. Gareth has recently launched a new podcast together with Richard Willet called WTAF (What the Actual Fuck) where they cover topics critical to these times of great change and join the voices of rebellion across the planet.

These names are a few of the incredible, courageous people who are on the front lines, and they continue to inspire me to be the same. Dr. Judy Mikovitz, Dr. Sherri Tenpenny, Sterling Hill, Gareth Icke, and Ted Kuntz: THANK YOU!!! YOU are my HEROES!

On March 20, 2021, I had the honour to emcee The Worldwide Freedom Rally in Kelowna, BC, where we had over 100 cities and 50+ countries participate. It was a remarkable experience to BE a part of the energy that was created globally that day! I knew I was doing what my heart had called upon me to do.

First There Was the WORD

I am reminded that I may one day have to look into the eyes of a child that asks me, "What did you do to fight for my rights and freedoms?" I want to look right back in love and truth and say, "I did everything I could, to the best of my ability, to make certain you knew what it was like to BE FREE!"

There is something significant that happens within you when you follow your calling (even when it's super uncomfortable). I'm adaptive and bend like the willow in the wind. I have learned to be comfortable with being uncomfortable because the generations that are coming after us are counting on us! It is important to me that I make my best contribution and leave here knowing I did everything I could to make a difference and impact someone's life.

FREEDOM has always been my "word". Those that are in my inner circle know I speak often and loudly about the power of words. Right beside freedom is happiness. I remember during one of my darkest moments a friend asking me what I really wanted in my life. My response: "All I want is to be happy". That moment has never left me. I AM a very different woman compared to a year ago -- hell, even to a day ago -- as each and every moment continues to shape me and hone me into the woman I choose to become. Another layer of magnificence unfolds. I'm peeling away at the onion, so to speak, to rise to my infinite potential.

Health and Wellness

Outside of going to the hospital for broken bones and stitches, I have never really been sick. I recognize that my foundation of being a Saskatchewan farm girl and living off the land and eating food from soil that still held selenium has allowed me to age gracefully and stay strong. I have aligned myself with a conscious, health and wellness organization with integrity whose tagline is "Disruptive By Design". I love that, as I've always been a bit of a rebel and an "out of the box" thinker.

With everything that is taking place in the world, I know the importance of having a superior mind-body-soul connection. I have products that feed my body, provide cellular nutrition, and get the supplements to the places in my body that need them. I learned the importance of "it's not what you put in your body, it's what your body can absorb". If your cells are not healthy and strong to absorb the nutrients, what you are really doing is creating "expensive pee". Then we drink that water so YES, I speak of pure water, and I have a solution for that, too.

We are all created to be centurions, and I, for one, will be an example and role model for others.

Becoming More

I feel more powerful than I ever have. I have become empowered.

I have found my voice.

I have a sense of peace. Calmness during these uncertain times is a blessing.

I continue to build my global online business in the arena of health and wellness.

My teachings on empowerment, consciousness, well-being, and commerce continue to evolve.

I will always surround myself with like-minded, phenomenal human *BEcomings* who love me, encourage me, support me, and challenge me to BE more.

May we all continue to shine as the brightest light in the universe!

I'm a drop in the ocean.

Join me on this journey to take the ripples of our experiences and create tidal waves of greatness. It starts with me, and it starts with you!

Let's make this world a better place. After all, this is THE GREAT AWAKENING!

About Darlene Ondi:

Darlene Ondi has a drive for excellence. Known as the "Go-To" Person, her talents as Executive Coordinator for two global CEOs, supported her in working with women all over the world to yield a revenue of over $1 Million.

Currently, she is working to bring awareness to the world as an activist. She participates and facilitates freedom rallies where Canadians gather to defend their sovereign rights. Darlene is a magnet for high vibration people, one might call her an intuitive connector. Not only does she have a knack for bringing together collaborators of like-mind, she also is adept in tracking the details of production, to make sure the events achieve their goals. Darlene is a potent speaker, able to convey the important details with an uplifting vision and she has co-authored several books.

As a trusted colleague and valued liaison, Darlene assists with promoting and providing impactful and insightful collaborations. She recently emceed an historic assembly in Canada, and works closely with exceptional peers such as Ted Kuntz, President of Vaccine Choice Canada, Tanya Gaw of Action4Canada, and David Lindsay of C.L.E.A.R. (Common Law Education and Rights) initiative.

She has been an invaluable guest scout and liaison for 'The Other Side of the News.'

Darlene believes in freedom, empowerment, and BEing your highest most magnificent self. Working on a project dealing with OBEs, NDEs and other "out of the box" experiences, she reminds others that to come from a place of truth, compassion, and happiness are virtues to strive for.

Through a destined meeting, Darlene met Brian Condie and his wife, Crista who were live streaming the March 20th Worldwide Freedom Rally in Kelowna, BC where she was emceeing. Today they are creating The Mad Watcher TV 2.0 and the Ondi Condie Show to assist in getting truth out to the greater community and declaring the real heroes and warriors of this time!

Darlene radiates health...and so, people seek her out to learn how they too can enjoy health and wellness. Through her own journey, she has come to understand the importance of good nutrition and on a deeper level, one's beliefs, that "as a man/woman thinketh, so he/she is."

Darlene is about helping people and she lives by two mantras...KNOW THYSELF and TREAT OTHERS AS YOU CHOOSE TO BE TREATED!

BE the Change YOU wish to SEE in the world
~Ghandi

Chapter Three

The Sin of Silence

By Matt Belair

The world is a big and beautiful place. When I was younger, I knew I wanted to travel the world in search of some of the greatest masters and leaders the world had to offer. As a lifelong martial artist, it was a dream to train with Shaolin Monks in China.

The question "What am I capable of and what are humans capable of?" has been with me my entire life. What are the limits to human potential?

These questions took me to over 20 countries where I sought out masters in their fields. I meditated with monks in Nepal and survived a near death experience trekking Mount Everest. I trained MMA in Thailand and with 34th Generation Shaolin Monks in China who were legitimate superhumans.

This search took me to Egypt and led me to learn from three different Native American elders. One side of the search was about how one lives a good life, and the other side was "How come there is so much suffering on this planet and what can we do about it?"

After travelling the world when the pandemic struck, I found myself in my hometown of Cambridge, Ontario with a six-month-old daughter.

In my research, in trying to understand how the world was all connected, it was already clear that there were power structures and systems of which most of the population was completely unaware. In my twenties, I tried to tell my friends about what I was researching, but everyone was too busy with their own lives to care about some sort of global "conspiracy."

When the lockdown happened, that's when I knew this was serious and I began researching. It took about two weeks of full-time research to discover the intent and players behind this global *scamdemic*.

My life path took me from high performance coach for athletes, author, and vagabond to podcast host that allowed me to interview some of the greatest minds on the planet. I began using that platform to speak out about what was happening.

It was an incredibly disheartening experience to see how many close friends did not want to have a discussion. They labelled me part of the problem and would never have a rational conversation. I lost many friends that I had had for a lifetime. It was a battleground on all platforms until I got deleted from Facebook and Instagram in June 2020. I was one of the first accounts to go, and my posts were getting more shares than anything I had ever produced.

One of the research pieces was on Bill Gates, and another was on the collateral damage of lockdowns. Both posts got over 400 shares, which is astronomical compared to the usual 2 to 10 I would get when posting a podcast.

The research I did came from peers who would link me to reliable sources. We would share and uncover old documents and documentaries and go right to the source. The Swiss Propaganda institute did a great job of tracking the analytics, and the hive mind of independent researchers did a phenomenal job finding original sources. I was also fortunate to be a part of a few groups on Telegram. One of these groups consisted of 100 doctors from around the world who would go through the data and ensure we would all see and understand the truth behind the propaganda.

Some of my major passions are consciousness, mindset, and human potential. This led me to study persuasion, beliefs, programming, self-hypnosis, brain science, and many other similar topics. In this search, I also came across how the elite use propaganda, brainwashing, and psychological warfare on its own people, with incredible results.

You can look at the Rwanda genocide, for example, or watch the documentary *Century of Self* about Edward Bernays. The art of psychological manipulation has been pretty well mastered by the elite. In today's age, it's even more effective because they can use television, celebrities, radio, social media, and various other platforms to spread propaganda. This worldwide hoax would not have been possible without the internet because they wouldn't have been able to keep it in our faces.

In understanding that there are small groups of people who rule this world (for now), it always seemed too big to solve. I didn't know how to end hunger, stop war, or create peace, even though I had an understanding of how they were being manufactured.

When this started, there was no choice but to speak out because the plan was so evil that I would be ashamed of myself if I did not do everything I could to be a part of the solution.

When so many people of influence decided to remain quiet, that was another gut punch. There were a lot of people who had large followings and influence in the fields of health and wellness, personal development, and spirituality, and almost all of them chose to remain silent.

Those of us who did speak out were deleted, banned, shadow banned, and slandered in the first technological book burning in history. We learned that big tech and social media are enemies of the people and need to be eliminated or regulated to ensure corruption is not possible.

In a few short months, my work of five years was almost wiped from the record. My Facebook account was deleted with my travels, and even personal accounts were deleted, along with my Instagram account with over 40,000 fans that I had grown from years of podcasting and teaching about consciousness, spirituality, performance, and human optimization. All of this was because I wanted to know the truth about the coronavirus and how deadly it was.

When we knew the survival rates were incredibly high, the brainwashing had already kicked in. And so, those who fell into the trap of fear could not listen to anything different. They awaited their saviour, the vaccine.

The decision to spend the past year dedicating my life to finding the truth and sharing it as far as possible has cost me friendships, has almost deleted years' worth of work, and it has caused financial challenges. And this is still just the beginning. The truth is that it isn't even a choice. It's something an honourable person must do in the face of tyranny.

What I may "save" by remaining silent is not nearly as important as what I will lose as far as spiritual integrity. This is a spiritual war.

There is a famous saying that says, "Fear is the mind killer." This entire sham can only live in fear, deceit, and deception.

We must understand fear and learn how to overcome it. In working with extreme sports athletes, fear is a constant element they have to overcome to perform at their best. Anyone can use the same tools to improve their own life.

The first thing is to accept reality as it is. Do not distort what is happening in your mind. Once you are aware of the situation, you can then gain the knowledge necessary to find a solution. Most fear comes from lack of knowledge. For example, I would be terrified on the open seas in a sailboat, whereas a sailor would be right at home because they have the knowledge necessary to survive.

A common misconception about fear is that you shouldn't feel it, or some people don't feel it. Being fearless means having one more unit of courage than fear. If you are 100 units scared, you need 101 units of courage to act. Bravery and courage are feeling and experiencing fear but doing what is right anyway.

Faith is another important element to overcoming fear. If you know that you are part of something greater, if you know there is a God, creator, or spirit that you are a part of, then you have less fear of death. Since I have had several near death experiences, this is a knowing for me. You can also have that knowing with an honest seeking of and connection to whatever your higher understanding is.

Each day is a new gift, and life is not promised. When we die, the mirror will come up on our lives and we will judge ourselves. So many will be disappointed in themselves when they realize how much they lived in fear. Courage can be earned step by step. Start with small acts and over time being courageous will be your natural way of being.

It is time for all of us to grow up as individuals and as humanity. There are dark forces on this earth, and they will be overcome when the people move out of fear and begin to participate in building a better world together. When we have our individual knowing and connection to spirit, God, and the universe, we can live in peace and harmony with ourselves. When we are able to do that, we shift our thinking from "what can I get?" to "what can I give or how can I help?"

We also move from the victim mentality to a mentality of self-responsibility and capability.

The only way that this world begins to shift in a positive way is for each of us to find our own power, connection, and truth. To be guided by our hearts and spirits. To do what is right and not what is easy.

In the Bhagavad Gita, it says that most people believe violence is when you harm another man or woman. But when you live in the realm of "maya", or illusion, and you do not offer the truth to your fellow man, you have committed violence.

We are in the biggest deception in history. This is a global de-population event. This is not my opinion; it's in their literature. You can view Georgia Guidestones for reference.

In studying Law the last few months, it's very fascinating to know that the 1611 King James Bible is what the queen swears her oath on. It's also true that those evil people who are pulling the strings often define themselves as Luciferians. Lucifer is a deceiver, but he still requires your consent.

That is why when you put your faith and trust in God, spirit, or the Creator, in whatever that is for you, you'll be guided and supported.

We all have to walk this path on our own. It's a solo journey where we must speak, act, live, and breathe with integrity, service, kindness, and compassion. Be the example we want to see so that we know we are doing our part.

This system wants you to believe you are alone, weak, and the minority. It wants you confused and looking for a "savior". You are stronger than that. Be your own saviour and know that there are millions of people around the world who support you and are proud of you for doing the right thing.

It makes sense that there are even spiritual realms that are watching and are a part of this awakening process. With great challenges and tragedy come great opportunities.

One great quote to guide you when seeking the truth is from Rudolph Steiner, "Anything that seeks to restrict or bind, by definition, is Luciferian".

When you are seeking the truth and someone wants to impose their beliefs on you by forcing you to do something, you can know for sure it does not come from God or the truth.

We are in a spiritual war. It can be scary at times, but remember you are an infinite being and life does exist beyond this realm.

Do not sell or compromise your soul for ANY reason.

Put your faith in yourself and in God. Grow your faith and do what you can to be the best person you can be. You don't have to save everyone; you just have to do your part to find your own power and your way back home.

That will leave the light for others to follow.

About Matthew Belair:

Matthew Belair is an author, athlete, coach, and speaker who's on a mission to empower people to master their mind, body, and spirit and make the world a better place.

Matt hosts the Master Mind, Body and Spirit Show, which has reached #1 on iTunes in over 20 countries. He has interviewed hundreds of the world's foremost experts on consciousness, spirituality, and peak performance.

He empowers his community with teachings and strategies that focus on helping expand consciousness, finding purpose, and achieving highest potential.

He is the bestselling author of *Zen Athlete: A Guide to Self-Mastery* and *Zen Athlete Training Program*. Matt's mission is to make training for the mental game of sport go mainstream and empower future generations with critical knowledge around mindset, performance, and personal empowerment.

Matt Belair is a student, researcher, and explorer. He has been trained in intensive meditation with Tibetan monks in Nepal, trained with professional MMA fighters in Thailand, and with 34th generation Shaolin monks in China. He has also trained and studied with Native American Elders and attended a trip to Egypt with the Resonance Science Foundation exploring both ancient civilizations and advanced technologies.

Matt is a thought leader in consciousness, spirituality, mindfulness, and peak

performance. He has a global audience and has been featured on many top podcasts and magazines.

https://mattbelair.com/

Chapter Four

Truth Warrior

By David Whitehead

My background: I am a life-long truth seeker who was born in Calgary in 1982. I've lived in Ontario, Saskatchewan, Ontario again, and now in beautiful BC. I love this country dearly and have toured coast to coast a few times now.

I grew up with an interest in the martial arts, philosophy, history, and "fringe" subjects. My interest in martial arts, which started at the age of nine, led to a career as a self-employed business owner where I have run my own dojo/fitness practice with my wife since 2008. We both quit our corporate full-time jobs and decided to become full-time entrepreneurs instead. We built a great business and community in Toronto and on the West Coast. That all came to an end in March 2020 when, due to "emergency health orders", we were forced to close our doors, and our gym facility was converted by the city into a homeless shelter.

Sadly, as of this writing, there is no foreseeable way to open up again since the government can virtually shut us down at any moment they please and with little warning or justification. Our estimated losses from closure till now are between $80,000 and $100,000 in revenue. When it happened, I swore to myself and my family that I would not accept a single penny from this utterly incompetent government. I have been true to my word. I was fortunate to have also started a small part-time online website business back in 2016, to which I turned my full attention after getting shut down literally overnight. We were able to build that up to a point where we could make do on our own, but it was hard. We had just closed on our new dream home two weeks before the lockdown. A few weeks after that, my mother passed away due to heart failure. I was unable to go and visit or see my father or my family due to travel restrictions. I have yet to see them. I ended up doing a private live funeral podcast in her memory for my loved ones, as it was the best I could do at the time. I had to put aside my grief, my anger, and my frustration, and get to work on channeling that into productivity and my podcast. I am happy I did. I have produced my best work to date during all of this.

I have been expecting this global lockdown or something similar for some time. I did not know when, or in what capacity, they would do it, but I have been awake to the globalist agenda since 2002 and have been researching intensely ever since. An event of this magnitude was looming. As a matter of fact, 9/11 woke me up, as it did so many. It was the catalyst to a deep dive of research. I witnessed lie after lie by the media, after listening to so many testimonials from decorated engineers.

I have always known the mainstream media was compromised. I saw (and still see) a need for true journalism to return, not this glammed fake news charade. I sought to become the media I wanted to see out there. I started a YouTube channel and a Facebook account back in 2007 for the purpose of speaking out and sharing knowledge and have been covering numerous subjects on those and other platforms ever since. I had a following on those channels of around 35,000. I worked very hard for years to gain that following. My work in this got me on radio and on several TV spots on History Channel, which eventually grew into my own production projects. My personal show is called Truth Warrior, and I also do a collaborative project called Unslaved with Irish Author/researcher Michael Tsarion. After I started my public work, my research became a life mission that I did in my spare time. After 2020, it became a full-time job, and I am eternally grateful for it. I was demonetized and shadow-banned first by various social media, and then eventually permanently shut down on Youtube, Facebook, Instagram, and Spotify. All within three weeks of each other. This was due to my being outspoken about the global lockdown and government policies. This banning ended up almost destroying my ability to earn income with my work as I no longer had access to my hard-earned following. I then had to rebuild on censor-free platforms and completely restructure my business in a very short period of time in order to survive. Which I did. I am grateful every day that I found the right people, the right teachers, the right platforms, and the right information exactly when I needed it. I am now all-in.

My mindset before 2020 was that it would just be business as usual, keeping an eye on world events that would slowly move us all towards the centrally-planned global government/ economic system. According to the research I had done up to this point, the globalist elites had been working towards achieving their dark agenda for decades, if not centuries.

After the "pandemic" hit in March of 2020, something inside me knew this was not at all what they were saying it was. I honestly didn't know what it was, but I dug in to see if I was just going crazy or not. As I looked at what I could find at that time, it appeared to me as though someone had just hit a giant green button somewhere and decided to rush this agenda/experiment ahead using this pandemic as the excuse. I had to confirm this for myself, as anyone even whispering such an idea would be thought insane or paranoid. I didn't sleep much in those early months. I feel I have since confirmed this hunch as I decided to put in full-time hours researching what was really going on, and to report my findings to my audience and network. I learned much from the numerous interviews I conducted during 2020/21 with top experts and researchers from many diverse fields and from all around the world. I was able to salvage most of these interviews in a playlist on my Rokfin channel entitled: "Corona Chronicles."

I will continue this work because I know our freedom, our children's futures, and our very existence are all at stake.

I decided years ago to start speaking up because I told myself that if I didn't, who would? I had the public speaking ability from my years as a martial arts coach, and I had access and connections to, in my opinion, some of the greatest researchers, authors, and minds of our time through my podcast. I felt I owed a debt of 'paying it forward' and I had also acquired the technical knowledge of how to produce digital content. I have dedicated myself fully to this mission of seeking truth, freedom, and justice ever since.

I get my information from a variety of sources from both past and present that are a mix of mainstream, alternative, insider connections, whistleblowers, fellow journalists etc., and some of it is also experiential. Knowing who or what to believe is a combination of hard work in vetting and confirming information as well as is possible and trusting one's intuition and synchronicity. In short: a combination of mind, heart, and gut. There must be multiple confirmations before I will present it. I also keep it an ongoing study as new information comes out all the time and I realize how impossible it is to have access to everything at once. Unlike our (s)elected officials and media teleprompter readers, I believe firmly in the real scientific method of investigation. I also believe in telling the truth even if it costs me. I also have built an amazing network of fellow citizen journalists that assist me in discovering and sorting through various leads, stories, articles, books, and bits of intel.

My relationships with friends and family on one hand have indeed suffered due to my pursuit of the truth, however on the other hand I have built lasting friendships and alliances this past year with some of the best people I now know and that would not have come about under any other circumstance. I am very grateful for that.

By speaking my opinion and research freely, I have lost many opportunities in life and in business. I have lost two businesses, a television career, many friends, most of my family doesn't talk to me anymore, and I have been harassed and threatened on many occasions. Good thing I learned to have a spine through other hardships early on in my life. The martial arts philosophy and background taught me discipline, courage, and humility. There is no room for lies in combat. I have taken those lessons with me as I do this work. I feel I was prepared for this in advance. Every loss I have suffered has now transformed into another gain. I now know that I have learned many valuable lessons during this global event and have enriched my mind and spirit to a degree that could only be possible under this kind of tremendous pressure and opposition. My resolve is ironclad. Before, I still had my doubts about what I could do. For this, too, I am grateful .

My main mediums of communication right now are my podcasts, my social media channels such as Telegram, Gab, and Twitter, and my face-to-face conversations with people in my community.

The one thing I had to learn early on, and am still learning, is the use of discernment. I realized a while back that you are only as good as your information. So I started focusing a lot of time on my own personal development and overall mental and physical health so that the best and clearest signal could come through while I conduct my work and research. I am not perfect at this by any means, but I do my very best to remain honest and objective in my pursuit of the truth. I believe that there is the truth, and then there is my and everyone else's opinion. If history teaches us one thing it is that more often than not, we humans are wrong -- especially 'the experts' of the day. It is the truth that is always right. So, I started using a phrase in my podcasts and posts: TRUTH WINS. I believe this wholeheartedly and aspire to align with what is, not with what I think something is or wish something is. Only what it truly is. I strive to pass this concept on to those who will listen.

I am going to come out and say it: Canada is in big trouble. It didn't start with the pandemic. It started well before 2020. However, it is not a problem that is insurmountable. We don't even need everyone to wake up to the truth about what is really going on. What we need is to take hold of what Margaret Mead once said: "Never doubt that a small group of thoughtful, committed citizens can change the world. Indeed, it is the only thing that ever has."

The People of Canada and the world need to think about what they really want. Maybe we didn't really know what we wanted (or didn't want) until we were pushed to the edge of the precipice like this. Perhaps that is what is going on here on the larger cosmic level of all of this. We do live in a duality, after all. Evolution of any kind can only happen with the grinding pressure of opposing forces. I often think of the intense process of how a swordsmith makes a perfect katana blade. It takes fire, steel, pressure, and lots of hammering in order to be forged correctly. Your muscles only grow stronger after you tear them through the process of hard strenuous work in the fields or in the gym so they can rebuild. Your thinking can only expand when you challenge your mind on a regular basis. It is never automatic. Yet here we have been thinking and believing that it was automatic. Boy, were we wrong?

We are not getting what we want right now, but we may be getting exactly what we need: a massive wake-up call. Do we want the illusion of security provided by a heavy-handed and grotesquely corrupt state made up of compromised individuals who hold other allegiances than to you or this country? Or do we want freedom, real health, and prosperity? What I have learned is that freedom, like health, is earned. It is not given. The world will never give you freedom. That is a gift that you give yourself. Freedom also requires courage -- the courage to take a stand while everyone else around you complies without a second thought or runs and hides. Courage can only grow inside you when you love. It requires that you love yourself, your life, your family, and your freedom so much that you are willing to sacrifice temporary comfort and instant gratification in order to defend it and preserve it. We don't have to "die" in some great revolutionary struggle. Today's war is a spiritual war, and a war on consciousness more than anything else. The part of ourselves that holds us back from being our true, great, and best selves must die. If it is true that fear is produced in the mind due to the absence of knowledge, then it would serve us well to reclaim our minds and work towards gaining knowledge of the truth, no matter how scary it might be. Clarity repels fear, even when it's scary. Only when our worst fears are faced and defeated can healing begin.

Another great quote that has stayed with me is: "If you don't control your own mind, someone else will." This is a fact that stares us all in the face right now.

Miyamoto Musashi once said: "Truth is not what you want it to be; it is what it is, and you must bend to its power or live a lie."

A similar statement with a slight twist was made by Jiddu Krishnamurti: "It is truth that liberates, not simply your effort to be free."

Basically, only the truth will set us free. It can't come any other way. Some would say we had more freedom before 2020. But did we really? Did we have connection to and concern for the truth before 2020? Clearly, not as much as we perhaps thought, seeing as everyone fell so easily for the lie that could condemn us all to a new kind of slavery never before seen in human history. Is this why we are now losing our freedom? This is why, in my humble opinion, we must put the pursuit of the truth before all else as we seek to reclaim our freedom and humanity. Not the truth that we cherry-pick or prefer, but the whole truth, as it is in all its glory and horror. We have all probably heard, and told, enough lies to know the difference. Remember that the truth is always at war with the lie. A lie must be believed in order for it to have power. That alone tells you how much power you DO have. You have the power of choice and free will regardless of what the world around you does or doesn't do. Which means we need WARRIORS for truth to rise up now. We need strong individuals to find their inner power and let their voices be heard. We need those on the inside of this control system who fear reprisal, loss of job, loss of social status, etc., to also find the courage to speak up now. You will be heard, and you will be supported. As the saying goes: "Speak the truth, even if your voice shakes." I believe that unseen forces come to aid those who do so, and justice will come for those who do not.

A comment about fear: We always fear what we don't understand. That's exactly where the 'powers that (shouldn't) be', want. Not in fear in the way you might first think, but in deep and constant ANXIETY. Fear comes and goes. Anxiety stays with you. That level of fear is only possible in a mind that is not free. The only pandemic afoot in my estimation is a pandemic of mass hysteria and mono-mania (insanity conceived as single pathological preoccupation in an otherwise sound mind.) Knowing this gives you the solution. We have been given an opportunity to face all of our fear and anxiety and to cure it with courage, knowledge, and understanding.

A few questions I asked myself when I realized what we faced: What will you do now? What can you do? What are your talents? What connections do you have? What skills do you have? What are your strengths? Those questions brought me to the work I am doing now, and I believe it IS having an impact. At the very least, it has helped me through this time.

If you have a beating heart and a love for your life, your family, and your freedom, you can find a way to be a part of the greatest awakening ever recorded on this planet. You can find a way to survive and to win in this life. This is YOUR life. No one passes through the gates of your mind or your life unless you allow them to. Make this a study. Be an observer of what is happening. Take the action your heart, not your fear, tells you to take. In the end, I encourage you to be on the right side of history. I hope you will join myself, and literally hundreds of millions around the world, on this mission to awaken ourselves and the world. You are not alone. This can be won. This will be won because it MUST be won. In the end, TRUTH WINS.

About David Whitehead:

David is a full-time podcaster, martial artist, coach, entrepreneur, and public speaker with a lifetime of study and interest in esoteric information, philosophy, comparative religion and mythology, ancient and modern mysteries, the paranormal, and current geopolitical events.

He is an independent researcher with a personal quest to seek out the answers to many of the challenging questions of our time and he hosts his own show, *Truth Warrior,* where he covers these subjects in detail. He has been featured on The History Channel's *Ancient Aliens* and *UnXplained* and is also the director/co-host of the popular podcast *Unslaved* with Irish Author/Researcher Michael Tsarion.

https://www.dwtruthwarrior.com

Chapter Five

The Great Social Experiment

By Owen Owen Owen

Since early March 2020, I have devoted 7,000-plus hours of independent research. Yes, I have much to add to this current conversation, and I have some solutions for anyone who is stuck in the dilemma we call "The Great Social Experiment of 2020."

Both sides of my family have interesting histories. I am a direct descendant to Owain Glyndŵr (Welsh Braveheart) on my father's side and a direct descendant to both General Wolfe and General Montcalm on my mother's side. Conflict, action, and fighting oppression are built into my DNA and I will fight for what is right until my last breath.

My parents taught me that "no question is considered a dumb question if you don't know the answer" and "always follow your gut, but make sure brain is in gear before mouth is in action". We learn from asking questions. Yet, many are afraid to. Quite the opposite, I AM ME, and I'm very capable of reading between the lines. I am relentless when it comes to finding the truth and am a stats and facts freak!

When "The Great Social Experiment of 2020" hit last March, many questions immediately came to mind, but two immediately stood out:

1. Cui bono?

2. With bodies allegedly falling in the streets of Wuhan, why didn't they shut down the world as

> soon as possible? Windows would be nailed shut, with decontamination chambers on all exterior doors, and our food/supplies would be delivered to us by the military in hazmat suits and full facial respirators. We wouldn't be allowed outside.

The problem? Only Wuhan reported the alleged dead bodies in the streets. Then it skipped the rest of China and wound up in Italy. An obvious question was: "Why was this not happening elsewhere in China?" Italy wasn't reporting "bodies on the street". Over the last 15 months, how many bodies have you seen in the streets? Enter the media. The media loves and preys on your fear. They make billions from your fear and will push the fear narrative to keep their ratings up at the expense of increasing your cortisol levels.

With this in mind, I reached out to my scientific/medical friends/acquaintances (300-ish in 20-plus countries) and started asking lots of questions for clarity. Of note, as a child, I had many health issues which were "gifted" to me from a vaccine, including respiratory complications, hypersensitivity, and allergies to pretty much everything. The first 18 years of my life were spent either in the doctor's office or in a hospital two to three times per week.

Fear porn took over my Facebook feed. On April 6, 2020, I created a public group, *Critical Thinkers of the World Unite, for* myself and a few of my friends to create an open dialogue. It grew to over 1,300 people in 20-plus countries with zero marketing. The group went through its fair share of growing pains and a handful of trolls at the beginning. Now? It runs smoothly without the trolls.

The internet is a vast resource of information, but you have to know how to use it. In 1994, I educated many general managers, presidents, and CEOs on the importance and relevance of email and websites. In 1995, I was a part of worldrecords.com, which was the world's first music-related search engine.

I know search engines and Google have fallen from grace before, since they went public, to what we now call a "content creation engine". Unless you are looking up an addy, restaurant, or sports scores, look elsewhere. When it comes to sensitive topics, i.e. the facts, they are buried many pages in, and the average person only looks at the first page of their search results. Me? I look at the first 15-20 pages or until I find what I'm looking for.

It gets worse. Not only are they, YouTube and Facebook, watching your keystrokes, but they integrate your searches with predictive text/typing. I firmly believe that they are watching or listening in as I've had conversations when the computer was on and all of a sudden, I type in the first letters of a word, numbers for a street address, or a product, and boom, it autofills even on my first search. The same has happened to my partner.

There are alternatives, and although DuckDuckGo is starting to slip a little due to "bots", they are still better than Google.

OK, back to my story. During my time in the *Critical Thinkers Group*, I was exposed to a ton of excellent info and noticed that when I shared it on my personal page, the Virtue Vultures would appear and try to discredit the info I shared by verbally attacking me. Note, I make a point of only sharing source-based materials and avoid the "meme" garbage unless the sarcasm level is set to "stun".

Sadly for the haters, I don't back down and will never back down. I trust the sources, as they are referenced right from the "horse's mouth" or from actual experts who know what they are talking about and are not currently on the government payroll or directly from medical/scientific journals. We need perspective.

I took heat, abuse, and even a couple of death threats from my "friends". My best friend of 40 years, who became an EMT (2 years) won't talk to me anymore, and I had about 20 more unfriend me because I drew a line in the sand. However, one of my childhood friends is with OSHA (15-plus years), sits on the Infectious Disease Control Board in another province, and supports my findings and the science or lack thereof, especially when it comes to masks.

What I never expected was the number of new friends I have made through speaking out: 600-plus. The amount of private messages, texts, or calls I receive thanking me for making a stand is incredible. The stories are all similar when it comes to avoiding confrontation with their family or friends. This needs to change and only you can be the change, but you have to put the work in, and you have to be confident with your stance by putting the work/effort into reading and understanding the research. It's not rocket science and if I can do it, anyone can. Yes, it is that easy. Put ego and emotion out of the conversation. If you don't know how, ask someone who is achieving success or watch how they reply on social media or in person.

My involvement with Global Frontline Nurses has opened many other doors for me and provided me with lots of additional insight, facts, and perspective. What they are witnessing or have witnessed will blow your mind. Also of note, all of my research is on the website and is heavily vetted.

Summer of 2020 was brutal for everyone not named Bonnie Henry or in the government. She seemed hell-bent on cancelling summer even though we flattened the curve in early May like we always do, and I lost all of my major shows. For what? Well, I was able to play one show and it happened to be here in the Fraser Valley. We had 200 people in attendance. All ages, big pig roast/buffet, and not one person got sick or died. Odd? No, this is NORMAL.

However, as I mentioned above, I'm tenacious, especially when I know that I am being screwed over. I was livid.

It was time to go on the offence. Calls and emails - rinse and repeat!

1. Public Health Authorities (PHA) (all levels)

For the last 10-plus months I have called and recorded a majority of my calls to my local health authority, the BC Center for Disease Control (BCCDC), and Health BC, asking for their peer-reviewed evidence for "healthy populations wearing masks" and "healthy populations practicing social distancing". Knowing the corporate hierarchy works to my advantage, if someone couldn't answer my question, I would politely request , "Please pass me on to someone who can". You don't need to be an expert to ask these questions.

Results? "We have NOTHING"

Both the local health authority and the PHA would either say "we have nothing" or "check the BCCDC website". Now, what they didn't know was that I had already checked the BCCDC's website, and their "proof" was all based on anecdotal observations and models, aka low-level science. For your information, my calls usually last between 30 minutes to an hour, which turn out to be an education session. Sad, but true. They are so heavily compartmentalized that it is sickening, and these are the people who are supposed to provide you with the info. Not good enough!

As the months passed, the amount of research increased - masks, distancing, patents, lockdowns, etc. The more I read, the more I realized that my gut was right. Watching the regular fear broadcasts from the Public Health Office (PHO) was painful with the amount of flip-flopping they were spewing, plus the blatant lies and the lack of transparency when it came to their raw data, especially on hospitalizations and deaths.

Who was being hospitalized? The elderly? Did they have any comorbidities? What was the daily hospital census nationally and provincially? The same applies for deaths.

What many fail to realize is that our paid health "experts" have never seen a COVID patient but had no issue providing the data for positive test results from the labs. No data to explain duplicate test results. No answer for the amplification rate of the PCR, on which I blew the whistle back on Dec 23 after threatening Life Labs with a Freedom of Information (FOIA) request. It's 40 in BC. Also, we need to know from the "positive" test results who was sick and who wasn't sick.

One needs to pay close attention to their wording and facial expressions. Case in point: The non-pharmaceutical countermeasures they call "masks", and "social distancing" are not based on any high-level science. I was also amazed at how quickly the word "vaccine" was mentioned at the beginning, but more on that later. In fact, I mentioned this very issue to my group back in late April/early May 2020, which was really disturbing as this is the first time in my five decades on the planet where the medical community, as a whole, turned their collective backs on non-vaccine treatment protocols. Yes, you read that correctly, and yes there are many peer-reviewed studies for various combined therapies, with five randomized control trials for HCQ alone.

2. Don't be afraid of social media

Now I may get some flak for this, but hear me out. Social media can be your friend and there are a few secrets which have proven successful for me. Base your posts or comments with "source material". Avoid using the media as your reference unless you are pointing out the inconsistencies within their articles, and they have TONS!

Aside from hiding behind their posts by making others do their dirty work (replies), the media has a little problem when it comes to reporting the facts these days. They seem to exclude the actual study or source links when they say, "experts say" or "studies say". Well, where in the hell are the links to the studies?

As it stands, I get into 60-100-plus debates per day on the media's Facebook pages. Their articles are heavily biased to fit the narrative. So, I fight back with one or two sentences, "truth bomb", and see who attacks me. Many will reply with rhetoric which only shows their true ignorance. My follow-up replies are loaded with vetted sources and source links. Remember, Facebook allows 8,000 characters per comment and some of my replies are 10 or 15-plus comments.

Results? I rarely get a reply after, or I get blocked. I do get many kudos, likes, or personal messages thanking me. My findings are meant for everyone to use to their advantage, but you have to read them - fully.

3. Call your elected representative

Does everyone remember the Italian MP who verbally slammed his country's president? I do, and I have used this to my advantage. When it went viral, I sent a message to my MP with the video and a note saying, "It's a pity that politicians don't have a backbone when it comes to standing up for their constituents. Good luck getting re-elected ;)"

He replied back within an hour, and we were conversing within a couple of days once our schedules aligned. MPs only give you four minutes. For me? Thirty-plus minutes, as once I get going, I'm like a loaded freight train running down a steep hill.

My MLA experience was the opposite until after the snap election in October 2020. However, I found a loophole, which can be used both provincially and federally.

Back in Jan 2021, I started calling my MLA when Bonnie Henry started pushing the goal posts and, like you, I was pretty upset and frustrated. The first couple of calls were a pain as his "gate keeper" kept on asking, "What do you want to discuss with him?" My replies were, "Did I vote for you? No. And since I hate repeating myself and you are not MY elected official, kindly take my number and have him call me at his earliest convenience. Thank you". She continued with the verbal tennis match, and I stood my ground. Problem is he never called me back.

Well, that was until an unrelated call to the BC Ombudsperson for an unrelated matter wound us up talking about COVID.

Here's the secret: If you call a couple of times and do not get a call back, call again, and threaten that you will be "filing a complaint with the Speaker of the Legislative Assembly" (or whatever it is in your Province). For MPs it would be to the "Speaker of the House."

The results? He called me back in 10 minutes. After spending 30 minutes with him, I was horrified at the lack of information he was given from the PHO, who ONLY gets information from the CDC and WHO. Keep in mind that he was a lawyer before getting elected, and I stapled him to the wall when I asked what independent research he has done, where the 'risk benefit analysis' is, and what the province's 'exit strategy' is. He has since asked for my research.

4. Don't be afraid of businesses preventing you from shopping. Fiefdoms are illegal in Canada.

When the mask mandate finally arrived, a potential problem appeared: I can't wear a face mask for more than 38 seconds without triggering an attack. Fact.

As a former business owner, I've actually read the bylaws, my business license, codes, etc. You have to, as ignorance of the laws and facts is no excuse. The same applies to "orders" which are NOT LAW!

There is a reason why "exemptions" were added to every provincial mandate and pretty much everyone on planet Earth is exempt from wearing a face mask for day-to-day activities as both O2 deprivation drops by 18-22% within one minute, and Co2 increases by a factor of 10 within 45 seconds to one minute and it increases every 10 seconds.

Not everyone can wear a mask, and I have actually read every mask study, expert commentary, expert opinion, review, etc. from the 1920 Kellogg Study to present day. I published my findings for everyone to view on the Global Frontline Nurses website.

A short synopsis?

"Of all of the studies regarding face masks currently cited by various governments, health agencies, and media outlets:

1. Not one study they attempt to cite has "healthy people/populations" as a control group.

2. There are no peer-reviewed studies for "healthy people/populations" wearing masks.

3. There are no studies which have masks as the only form of source control (usually mixed with hand washing, sanitizer, or distancing).

4. Many of the references have no relevance to the actual study.

5. A majority of the above studies are based on anecdotal observations.

There is no reliable or policy-grade evidence that face masks can reduce the risk from COVID-19."

Remember, knowledge is POWER!

Like my experience with the "health authorities", I would ask to speak with the owner, manager, or anyone in executive management. Remember, it's your money, and businesses should be grateful to have YOU as a patron.

The calls were pretty easy for me because of all of my debates and my exhausting research. However, it is important to remain calm. This is critical for your success.

I would ask them if they read the provincial mandates, section 4 of said mandates. I would explain to them that I was a former business owner, I am not there to create any problems, and that I need to eat. I was also willing to shop later in the day to avoid creating any disturbances with other patrons.

However, I posed a very simple question:

"In the event that I have to wear a mask and something happens to me that either causes me or someone an injury or death because I pass out and either take someone down with me or take an aisle down and harm others, etc., who will be held liable?"

Their replies were all consistent. "That's an excellent question, Owen."

My reply: "Not good enough. Who will be held to account? Does your insurance cover issues like the ones I mentioned? Do you want to have this looming over your head?"

The other things I ask or state:

1. "Canada is a country and not a set of provincial fiefdoms, so please don't bring up the private property issues, and please refrain from using 'private property' as an excuse if you are leasing the building." The silence on their end to the above is hilarious.

2. "Where is the FIT Testing or Spirometry Testing for your staff or even your patrons?" There is a reason why the resource and construction sector and most healthcare professionals are tested twice a year. Once again, it helps to have close friends who are with OSHA/CCOSH.

My results? I have yet to wear a mask, and yes, I have four different health issues that exclude me from this experiment. A list of the companies I have gone after and won: Loblaws, Save-On Foods, Vancity, RBC, TD Bank, Canadian Tire, London Drugs, Home Depot, Rona (under their corporate umbrella), Meridian Markets, my local markets, our lawyer and accountant, Trek Cycles, T&T Auto Parts, Fuel Supplements, and Apple to name a few.

5. "Vaccines for COVID-19? Just say NO"

"Vaccines are the bargain basement technology for the 21st Century"
—Dr. Maurice Hilleman (1919-2005)

This is a huge concern for me, as a few of my health issues appeared when I was an infant and from the 2D's/2P's. I don't trust the vaccine manufacturers and I don't trust the government, so I'm making a stand.

As of this writing, I am involved in discussions with the Tri-Council Policy Statement (TCPS), Research Ethics Board, Office of Clinical Trials, National Institute of Health Research, and will be reaching out to all of the law societies regarding efficacy and informed consent as well. I have also created a *COVID-19 "Vaccine" Side Effects -- What's Really Going On?* group on Facebook with 1100+ members in under 5 days.

Now for the facts.

As per the 2011 Harvard Pilgrim study for which the CDC gave $1 million, the study found the following:

"Adverse events from drugs and vaccines are common, but underreported. Although 25% of ambulatory patients experience an adverse drug event, less than 0.3% of all adverse drug events and 1-13% of serious events are reported to the Food and Drug Administration (FDA). Likewise, fewer than 1% of vaccine adverse events are reported. Low reporting rates preclude or slow the identification of 'problem' drugs and vaccines that endanger public health."

https://digital.ahrq.gov/sites/default/files/docs/publication/r18hs017045-lazarus-final-report-2011.pdf

- Between 1955 and 2017, there have been 11 times where vaccines were pulled from the market with deaths between 25-50 people. As it stands, we are in the tens of thousands and well over one million have severe adverse reactions even though the VAERS system is almost four months behind.
- All of the five "authorized jabs" are not based on Canada, even though we have at least eight in clinical trials.
https://covid19.trackvaccines.org/country/canada/
- Only one (ModeRNA) did any form of trials for Phase 2 and Phase 3 but not enough numbers for Phase 3, which should be in the thousands or tens of thousands. We had allegedly 750, but that was in conjunction with the US for the same trial.
- Trials only tested healthy people (search for "Exclusion Criteria" in any of the "Vaccine" Manufactures FDA's reported documents.
- According to the Regulatory Services, if all of the regulation trials excluded a group of patients, we would never use that product in that group once it comes to market. Why? We don't know if it's going to work and we don't know if it's going to be safe. For pregnant women? They would or should never inject a

"biologically active substance" into a pregnant woman. Yet the first jab in pregnant women was done with NO KNOWLEDGE OF EFFICACY OR SAFETY DATA. The same applies to children and seniors, or anyone who didn't meet the "exclusion criteria", and that list is massive.

- Trials only showed the results after 14 days. What happened within the first seven days? Moderna? https://www.fda.gov/media/144434/download
- Trials did not address any of the potential severe adverse reactions to the October 22 FDA report on page 17. https://www.fda.gov/media/143557/download
- Health Canada's website states that vaccine approval takes ten years, plus there are usually two years to determine efficacy. We did COVID-19 in two months. Not good enough!
- All of the previous clinical trials for vaccines have required proof of serology, meaning that you are having an immune response stimulated in the body.
- All of them have required biochemistry as part of the clinical outcomes.
- This is the first time in ANY CLINICAL TRIAL where the intervention has been authorized, not approved on symptom mitigation alone, and this is not a standard that the FDA or any country equivalent can approve.
- Gene therapy based on what ModeRNA said in their SEC filings, plus they make it abundantly clear that the mRNA technology is considered by the FDA to be gene therapy. "Currently mRNA is considered a gene therapy product by the FDA. Unlike certain gene therapies that are irreversibly altering cell DNA and

could act as a source of side effects, mRNA-based medicines are considered gene therapies by the FDA and no mRNA product has EVER been approved by the FDA.

1. They are the ones that say that it's a gene therapy.
2. They are the ones that say that the FDA calls it a gene therapy.
3. They are the ones that say that there is no approval for mRNA products.

Remember, the definition of a vaccine has more to do with confirming immunity and resulting in antibodies that will keep you protected with a surveillance system. This is not that.

Even the WHO confirmed this back in 2016, reaffirmed this in 2018, and gave their guidelines on what a vaccine is:

- it actually blocks transmission (i.e. disrupts the transmission) of a virus or pathogen
- it stops someone from being infected
- or it may be a treatment of a disease meaning that it actually blocks the expression of a pathogen manifesting into a disease.

The clinical trials done by Moderna, Pfizer, or J & J did not measure any of those outcomes.

Therefore, this is a "medical device treatment" and it was set up for the clinical trials NOT TO MEET. In fact, the jabs are actually producing a pathogen which is a disease-causing entity. Yet the UK Health Department states that "COVID vaccines are the best way to protect people from coronavirus".

This is a blatant lie. There is nothing that is being injected into people that disrupts coronavirus, the virus. It is actually a way to turn your cells into a manufacturing mechanism to manufacture a pathogen, to which you then are allegedly supposed to build immunity.

Problem? We don't know if it actually disrupts anything about SARS-CoV-2, and we don't know that because it was never part of the clinical research.

Here's the loophole: Medical device treatments are not protected under the EUA, Interim Order, or Conditional Marketing Authorization.

I realize that there is a lot of information to process, but you can do something about this.

But what exactly?

A. For Vaccines? Start looking into "Notices of Liabilities", which you can serve via registered mail to your employer, jab administrator, doctor, your local health authority, provincial CDC, your provincial health authority, the PHO, your MLAs, premiers, MPs, etc. Notarizing them may be a problem. The solution? At least two witnesses.

B. Demand a public comment on the efficacy issues with your PHO and CMO.

C. For the non-pharmaceutical countermeasures (masks, distancing, and lockdowns) and the PCR testing? Also look into the Notices of Liabilities. Remember, these are "protected" under the Interim Orders (Emergency Use Authorization) and have not gone through the rigorous one-to-two-year testing performed by the FDA or any other version of the FDA anywhere in the world.

Remember, the first death was on December 31, 2019. The EUA was applied on February 3 without actual proof of isolation or purification of this alleged "novel" virus.

D. If you somehow get sick? Demand the therapies which have been proven to work, which are actually backed up by empirical data.

E. Don't live your life in fear. Speak your mind with confidence. Enjoy the moment. Don't worry about getting flak from your friends or family if they won't review ALL OF THE AVAILABLE EVIDENCE. And, yes, it is that easy. I'm still here and I'm not losing any debates I get myself into because I am informed.

YOU ARE NOT ALONE!!!

"The only way you can control people is by keeping them in ignorance. But as soon as a person becomes empowered with knowledge, nobody can control them when they are aware. They cannot be victimized once they are informed and once they've been empowered with knowledge."
— Fredrick Douglass

About Owen Owen Owen:

Owen Owen Owen is a professional musician/ independent researcher with 35-plus years of experience researching a wide variety of topics. His research is source-based only, and he spends upwards of 20 hours a day sifting through the available evidence, looking for clues.

Owen is also the founder of *Critical Thinkers of the World Unite* and *COVID-19 Vaccine Side Effects: What's Really Going On* (Facebook). He is also the webmaster/researcher for Global Frontline Nurses".

If and when he has time, Owen also is an advocate for various families nationally and for various groups during this "great social experiment of 2020". He goes after the corporations and government agencies head-on, without fear.

Owen is a former restaurateur, ski instructor, and talent agent, and he has held executive management positions in a variety of sectors including, but not limited to tech/communications, geomatics, water, health, resources, and finance. He is a stickler for facts and details and has spent over 7,000 hours doing independent research regarding COVID-19, from masks to social distancing, to lockdowns, to test kits, to patents, to copyrights, to clinical trials, and to the laws/order/etc. He is not here to tell you how to think or what to "believe" but to provide keys to various "locked doors" which are waiting for you to unlock.

www.globalfrontlinenurses.com

Chapter Six

What can I do?

By David Lindsay

Though born in Montreal, I was raised in Winnipeg. Winter cold and summer mosquitoes soon became the norm for living there for some 30 years. My youth was a mixture of active participation in off-road dirt-biking and motorcycle racing, gym workouts, cycling, and being a workaholic. Post Grade 12 education resulted in participation in a couple of unions, and regular non-union employment. Nothing spectacular until I was about 27.

I have generally always been anti-authoritative. This, I believe, provided an excellent foundation for my eventual participation in freedom-related issues.

I was fortunate, thanks to close friends at the time, to purchase my home in the outskirts of the North End in Winnipeg. I remained in this home until moving to Edmonton for four years at the request of a friend, and on the basis that it was better than Winnipeg.

This soon became a disappointment. I realized that the weather was much worse than Winnipeg, if this was possible, intercity travel was much more difficult, and so I decided to move to warmer climates. Such was my arrival to Kelowna around 2002. Fortunately, I have been able to remain in this beautiful area since. It was at this time of moving to Edmonton that I had to make the choice in life – freedom or stay in my home and go to work every day. I chose the former and had to give up my home.

While living in Winnipeg, I received, as did millions of other Canadians, an unaddressed mail from a Catholic publication in Rougemont, Quebec, called the Michael Journal. Though never being Catholic, an article on income tax piqued my curiosity. Three weeks after receiving it, I made the life-changing decision to read it.

Learning that someone had the belief that the *Income Tax Act* of Canada was unconstitutional was interesting. Fortunately, the author just happened to live in Winnipeg. I looked him up and arranged an impromptu meeting, which lasted for five hours. As a consequence, I purchased the book, *Call it Extortion*, involving the history of Winnipegger Gerry Hart, who, legend has it, refused to pay taxes for decades. Though the book contained some errors, fundamentally I later discovered it was and remains constitutionally correct.

In my late twenties at that time, my initial thought was of the riches to come for refusing to pay taxes. Due to the incredible information provided on the fraudulent banking system, and with guidance from others, I soon learned that the concept of becoming rich was not the issue – it was the corrupt banking system, which alone provided me all the reasons and information required to refuse to pay this corrupt tax.

I had learned enough at this time to realize if I was to quit paying taxes I had two options, as CRA would eventually come calling: either hire a lawyer (whom I already hated with a passion), or do the research myself, including in relation to legal procedures. I invested years doing research at law libraries in Winnipeg after work hours, including the courthouse and university, where the librarians were extremely helpful in assisting my research. My research led me to discover some fundamental truths about our constitution, our common law, equity, rights, liberties, the corruption of politics, and the right for every man to vote for his own oppressor.

Subsequently, to no surprise, I quickly learned of other rights and freedoms deprivations that have occurred, including the theft of our liberty to the free use of the public highways, and replacement with the privilege of driving with attenuating licences, registration, and insurance, all in name of, as with today, public safety being superior to our rights and freedoms. Such a philosophy is merely a form of socialism or communism, depending on how far down the leftist street one has traveled.

If there is one principle that I remember learning in school, and which has resonated in my soul throughout my freedom activist years, it is that our common law is based on the supremacy of the individual, NOT the collective. Collectivism = Socialism or Communism. Individualism = freedom.

I've always believed highways required three things to work properly: the ability to move quickly, safely, and efficiently. If any one of these were missing, the highways would fail in their purpose. As someone who has had repeated run-ins with the Winnipeg police enforcing safety over quick travel and efficiency (aka, speeding tickets), learning of the destruction of this liberty struck a real, raw nerve with me. The results of this work led me to write my first book, *Rights Denied*, demonstrating to many people the nature of our stolen rights and freedoms in this area.

During these formative freedom-oriented years, we arranged for weekly group meetings. They were great opportunities to meet like-minded people, but at this time, none of us really had the knowledge of how deep the corruption went, nor how to mount effective opposition. Many of our meetings became what I effectively referred to as "*bitch sessions*". But they did serve the purpose of getting many people involved in freedom who would otherwise have remained ignorant of these issues.

It is generally not possible to be active on freedom issues without at some point becoming involved in the court system. My involvement in the courts at all levels has been extensive. In one way or another, I have been in every court in seven different provinces, on my own or as an agent. I have filed five leave (permission) to appeal applications to the Supreme Court of Canada (SCC). All were denied, but after one year of demands, I was leaked an internal SCC document showing that only three applicants without lawyers were given permission to be heard by a full court, out of 900-plus applications. All the rest were lawyers, despite former SCC judges Binnie and Sopinka admitting that most lawyers do not know the test to have permission to appeal granted. The SCC will not allow unrepresented people to be heard, as a general rule. I met the test, admittedly in at least two of my applications, which involved everyone, for example, being charged transcript fees for appeals.

As mentioned, my involvement in the legal system has been extensive. Here are some examples:

My first involvement in the court system was in Winnipeg. I met two senior Canada Revenue Agency (CRA) (then Revenue Canada) officials who discovered a multi-billion dollar fraud in that organization (to no surprise, of course). Their story intrigued me, with their history of exposing the fraud and then finally quitting because of the ongoing corruption in CRA.

In the process, they attempted to lay criminal charges against government officials only to be stymied by corrupt court staff. I became involved and quickly obtained a secret internal judicial document, ordering justices of the peace to circumvent the *Criminal Code* provisions for private prosecutions. This practice immediately ended thereafter, though I was hated by all court staff as a result.

This led to my involvement in the criminal and provincial charging procedures and my ground breaking work, *The Annotated Criminal Charging Procedure in Canada*, which is the definitive book in Canada for everyone who wants to lay their own criminal charges, where the police refuse to do so, especially against government officials.

During this time, I successfully fought the attempts to bring in full searches at courthouses. I received over 1,000 signatures in less than a week at the Winnipeg courthouse, opposing this violation of our constitutional right of free, unimpeded access to our courts. I obtained all the court and government documents I could in relation to these searches and filed my own constitutional challenge – with a friend piggybacking beside me. I won at the Court of Appeal in a 2-1 split decision.

My involvement in freedom-related issues led me to new friends all over Canada. By my mid-thirties, it was clear that I had to flee the nest. During my stay in Edmonton, I began to help people charged with failing to file charges in the court system. After being accepted as an agent for a friend in the court, we arrived only to find seven police cars, strategically parked around the courthouse, spying on us.

Leaving the courthouse, my friend who was driving was pulled over for a driving infraction and gave the keys to me to hold. When I refused to give them to the police, I was arrested and charged with obstructing a police officer. Prior to the bail hearing, the officer forced me to wait while he had a ten-minute private chat with the Justice of the Peace! The JP refused to release me unless I agreed not to come into court unless required by law.

Weeks went by and I had to appear in court, as required by law, as an agent. This time, a swarm of police officers arrested me and charged me with breaking a court order. When I told the judge I was a court-accepted agent and was required by law to be there, they changed the release conditions so that I could only appear in court if I personally was charged with an offence! My second charge was thrown out, and a year later, the Crown stayed the first charge and kept this secret for another four months.

When I arrived to watch a court case, because I refused to have my knapsack searched in a Nanaimo court, the sheriffs physically pushed the judge out of the courtroom, claiming a security risk, while about ten sheriffs physically removed me and rammed my head against a concrete wall. All charges were again stayed by the Crown.

I then intentionally ran the B.C. Coquihalla Highway toll booth with friends to get a driving-without-licence charge. At first appearance, my case was put over by Judge Rhormoser until 2:00 p.m. During this time, I personally witnessed the judge going for lunch with the lawyer of another trial that was stopped for lunch. My demand for a new judge due to bias was denied by this same judge, so I walked out of court. A conviction was entered and I appealed.

I argued that charging for transcripts amounted to selling justice and was unconstitutional and contrary to Magna Carta 1215. Despite providing 20+ pages of authorities confirming Magna Carta was still part of our constitution, including the BC Court of Appeal in 1949; Justice Powers relied on a recent

BCCA case from a man who argued similar issues but provided no authorities at all, and denied my appeal for lack of transcripts. They knew the precedent this would set where governments would have to pay for all transcripts and judges would be prevented from using this as a method of blocking unrepresented people from coming to appeals court.

I then faced two incredible cases of failing to file income tax charges in Kelowna. Judge Sinclair failed in his duties to instruct me at that time (2004) for getting my evidence on the record, and my affidavits were never considered. Sinclair admitted he was getting instructions from "*those higher up the food chain*" to end my case – that's right, a pure admission of interference with the independence of the judiciary and my right to a fair and impartial trial. This left 50% of my case left off the trial record. To this point, my entire case rested on the Coronation Oath of the Monarch and the oaths of judges, and personhood, which were all ignored by the Crown and judge because my evidence never got on the record.

A conviction was entered and I was ordered to file tax returns. I refused, and I was charged again with failing to file a tax return from a court order. At trial, Judge Hogan commented that he thought I had used my defences in the previous trial. I replied that just because other judges broke the law, it didn't give him the power to break the law. He took his anger out on me with a 60-day jail sentence. However, no further orders to file were issued and no fine. The judge sent a clear message to the Crown that they did not want me back!

I also helped my friend in Ontario with the Court of Appeal on the basis that he had a constitutional right to have his own private smoking club. It was later discovered that a retired judge admitted to my friend that he interfered by pressuring the Ontario Court of Appeal judges to rule against us.

A senior Department of Justice official in Ontario admitted in a case that I was helping a friend with failing to file income tax returns, and that CRA was so scared of my success that they threatened to audit the judge if she ruled in our favour. The judge, who ordered me to provide a bill of costs after my submissions, as she was considering penalizing the CRA, did an abrupt facing and entered a conviction.

My instances in court include many more appearances, adjournments, motions, and applications, on my own and as an agent. I have had 37 counts of failing to file tax returns thrown out on my successful s. 11(b) application. (*s. 11(b) of the Canadian Charter of Rights and Freedoms guarantees that "[a] a person charged with an offence has the right...(b) to be tried within a reasonable time..."*)

Another nine such charges were thrown out on a successful trial case in 2019. I have helped many people successfully lower huge seven-figure fines and jail to little or nothing, and I have helped freedom activists get out on bail if charged, even at the Court of Appeal.

All this has come about from decades of research and sacrifices, resulting in very little personal life. It has resulted in being single for most of the past 25 years of my life. I have gone up against the worst criminals in the worst departments of our governments and judiciary. The COVID issue has completely divided my family to the point that there is virtually no relationship anymore, as they have been completely convinced, despite all contrary evidence, of a COVID pandemic.

Freedom is a multi-generational struggle, as there is always someone trying to steal our rights and freedoms away. The best we can do for our legacy is leave a community and nation in a better state than when we arrived. I don't expect people to invest decades of their lives in research and opposition to government corruption as I have done, in large part because most of the research has been done. People just need to learn it and live it. There will be sacrifices, but the alternative will be worse for your children than it was when you arrived. Doing nothing is an admission that rights and freedoms have little or no relevance in your life.

It is important to rid yourself of the fear and stigma of jail. For offences truly related to freedom, penalties at most are a fine or, rarely, a short jail term. As long as you pay any amount on your fine, they cannot jail you for non-payment. This may be a small sacrifice to show corrupt governments and judges that our rights and freedoms come first, not their corruption. Many peaceful people have spent time in jail for our beliefs and knowledge. Once governments and judges realize we are not scared of jail, they lose their power. I can attest to this first-hand.

I would recommend, despite property being a constitutional protection, that people make themselves judgment-proof. If you have a house, car, or anything else in your name, they will take it if you oppose them. Throw it back at them – own nothing and control everything. You can have an "*and*" chequing account (not, "*and/or*"). This creates a "*third person*" and prevents in most, if not all, cases bank accounts being garnished. Both people need to sign withdrawals, so you can order cheques and have one party sign all the cheques, and the other person can then cash them at will. Remember, it takes only 3% of the people to make a change – one person/house = 50% of the people. Change will happen.

The most important piece of advice I can share with everyone, especially in relation to the COVID issue, is to learn constitutional law, and to go directly to the source for information.

NEVER accept what any media tells you without verification. Most of their information is materially and significantly incomplete, if not outright false. But you may not know this if you do not understand constitutional law. On this point alone, most people are astounded to discover that the *Charter of Rights and Freedoms* is not our entire constitution. Indeed, even the *Constitution Act* of 1982 fails to encompass all of our constitutional principles, rights, and freedoms. This is materially beneficial to us – but we need to learn all sources of constitutional fundamentals, including case law, English documents (*Bill of Rights*, *Act of Settlement*, *Magna Carta*, and *Coronation Oath Act*).

If you learn that a government order was released, you need to get a copy of this order from the person (government website) who issued it, read and understand it, check the definitions sections, and determine loopholes and exemptions you can use and any legislation to which it relates. Yes, this requires you to learn a bit about law, but ignorance of law is the primary reason why we continue to have less rights and freedoms year after year. Similarly, never trust any report or medical study unless you have a copy of it and have read it. The prestigious medical journal *The Lancet* has already been caught publishing unverified and false medical studies in relation to COVID-19. No doubt more exist.

Sadly, every component of the judicial system has been compromised – left in place only because the judges take every opportunity to ensure justice is "*seen to be done*", but behind the scenes, reality is usually much different. Many decisions are made on judicial boardroom tables before the judge even enters the courtroom. The hearing/trial is a façade. We expect this politically, but it surprises people to hear that this corruption extends so deep into the very heart of the judicial system intended to stop this corruption.

Peaceful civil disobedience is the answer for those who truly believe in freedom. Complying with unconstitutional statutes/orders and complaining about it achieves nothing but instilling confidence in the corrupt government officials, that you will do as you're told, and that your rights and freedoms mean little. As Etienne de la Boetie noted 400 years ago in his book, *The Politics of Obedience*, the answer to corrupt governments is simple – Just say No.

Failure to say no is a licence to the State to impose tyrannical rights and freedoms deprivations upon all of us.

"Find out just what the people will submit to and you have found out the exact amount of injustice and wrong which will be imposed upon them;

and these will continue until they are resisted with either words or blows, or with both. The limits of tyrants are prescribed by the endurance of those whom they oppress."

— Frederick Douglass

Whereas peaceful civil disobedience is a fundamental right:

"A duty to a higher power confers a right against a lower power. If we owe a duty to God, then we have rights against the State.

The principle is recognized in the common law and was stated at Nuremberg: there comes a point where a man must refuse to answer to his leader if he is also to answer to his conscience."

The Spirit of the Common Law,

—Richard O'Sullivan Q.C. circa 1976 p. 76

About David Lindsay:

David Lindsay is a Canadian-born freedom activist and constitutionalist. He is self-taught over 25 years of activism, with respect to legal and constitutional issues, court procedures and preparation, and legal research. He is a co-founding member of the freedom-oriented and activist organization CLEAR – Common Law Education and Rights, based out of British Columbia, which is dedicated to the abolishment of the unconstitutional use of usury (interest) in our monetary system, and advancement and protection of our cherished rights and freedoms.

David has assisted dozens of other freedom activists in the court system, with a successful constitutional challenge to court security searches, a successful Charter application, and other trial successes in relation to rights and freedoms issues.

David is the author of *Rights Denied*, the authoritative legal work *The Annotated Criminal Charging Procedure in Canada,* and various publications educating on various aspects of the recent COVID-19 events.

Chapter Seven

Truth to Power

By Jason Christoff

My name is Jason Christoff. I was born in Turro, Nova Scotia, Canada. I moved at a very young age to St. John's, Newfoundland. In seventh grade, I then moved to Cornwall, Ontario, and I have stayed here most of my life. I graduated from McGill University in 1994 and opened my first business six months after graduating. Although I've led a comfortable life financially for most of my years, the injustices I've encountered and experienced have forced me to invest most of my time as a truth-teller.

At first, I spoke the truth into social media platforms when no one was listening. Even with very few listeners at first, I spoke the truth regardless. Soon a couple hundred souls started to hear me. Then a couple of thousand, then tens of thousands, and now hundreds of thousands visit my website every year. Responding to emails and providing interviews now takes up a good portion of my workday. The truth is in high demand. How did an entire culture get so far away from truth that only a choice few could speak it? Due to the fact that living truth brings pleasure and that living out a lie brings pain; you would expect that more people would be interested in pursuing truth. But here we are, a society drowning in lies and the pain that lies always bring -- a society in so much pain that truth is now being pursued like never before. The more people pursue the truth, the more the powers, that shouldn't be, also attempt to censor it.

I appreciate the tribe that has gathered around the Christoff campfire and I'm thrilled that the stories I tell now reach more and more people. We're all connected. We all want better. We all know we can do better. This is the dream of the truth-telling community. We bring the light. We bring the hope. We bring the dreams of a better tomorrow. We tell the truth. Our souls make us. We are here for a reason. Strong independent people don't need an artificial womb manufactured by the media and government to feel safe. We step outside the herd and say what needs to be said. Today the entire truth-telling community knows that we're in the fight of our lives. The best of humanity is now in a fight with a historical evil on this planet. An evil force from our ancient past, which is currently trying to reach out from its dark cave and snuff out the light. The truth-tellers are now the guardians of that light and we need more people to stand shoulder to shoulder with us.

The motivation behind what I do is simple. I don't want any child to experience what I experienced on this planet. At a very young age, I realized that I was constantly in fear, panic, and terror. It was a very powerful realization regarding the truth of our world. I was afraid of getting bullied and beaten up before, during, and after school. I was afraid of my neighborhood environment that was often immersed in conflict, chaos, and addiction. I was afraid of the mentally defective, pedophile priests at my grade school in St. John's, Newfoundland (called St. Bonaventures). I was afraid of the medical doctors in the white butcher coats who were always prescribing medical poisons for all my ills, when my very unhealthy "government approved" diet was the only thing making me sick. I was afraid of the politicians who constantly attacked the public under the guise of altruism and public health. I was most afraid of the morally weak, soulless, and childlike adults who were charged with the care of all the children, the innocent, and the defenseless. The moral weakness, in the vast majority of adults I encountered, acted as the catalyst for most of the abuses that my friends and I experienced in our youth.

This place was dark. I could see it. I called this place "planet mental asylum." It was beyond obvious. Every adult working in key positions of power seemed to gain greater financial rewards and larger occupational promotions the more they looked away from the complete trail of carnage and disaster that they created in their communities. This wasn't a good place to raise a child. I was that child, and very few people had the backbone to look these realities in the eye. In a society of weak, sedated, and addicted adults, the children suffer. At that point, it becomes a repetitive cycle that feeds itself, generation after generation.

It wasn't long until I started to ask myself, "What is this place, who are these people, and what am I doing here? Where is the joy, love, and compassion on this planet?"

To be honest, I still haven't answered those questions with any sort of clarity. What I have figured out is simple: Whatever this place is, it could use some improvement, to say the least. No child should ever be raised in such an environment. This sort of inverted bizarro stage show, run via a collusion between evil government and corrupt media, is growing worldwide. As Shakespeare once said, "Hell is empty and all the devils are here".

My writings and recorded lectures have discussed most every injustice and inversion I've seen during my short time here on this planet. Many of those writings can be found at www.jchristoff.com. Every day I witness the public being poisoned back into the stone age by a government gone mad, plus an endless fortification of media indoctrination, which continually disempowers the public at every turn. I see trusted institutions hiding behind veils of "public betterment", who in turn feed off the life force of an uninformed public. These corrupt institutions are destroying large tracts of our population where they stand, every single day. I see children absolutely incinerated by this system, as their parents have no idea that they're throwing their children onto the sacrificial fires due to inverted media conditioning, government brainwashing, and TV/movie mind control.

I would often look at the parents of my friends when I was a kid. These parents didn't like the jobs they were working; they were often addicted to caffeine, alcohol, or sugar; and they would waste large amounts of time engaging in activities that were counterproductive to their overall life success and happiness. Although it was obvious that the lives most parents were living held no capacity to provide them any long-term happiness or healthy outcomes, the parents would continually groom their children to follow in their footsteps. This ugly and rotting system is designed to produce a never-ending supply of loyal foot soldiers who feed their own children into this inverted and soulless energy extraction system. This mindless cycle, where intelligence and logic are completely gutted, has no ability to sustain any life form, society, or culture whatsoever. This system poisons and indoctrinates the public into complete dependence upon various levels of corrupt government, in order that this corrupt power structure "vampires" every last drop of life force from the host. This satanic system has always farmed us like milking cattle and now is looking at everyone as beef cattle.

This system produces nothing but misery, addiction, and soullessness for most. This is actually the design of the system. From cradle to grave, we are dumbed down and poisoned so we can offer very little resistance. Humans are just easier to rule, govern, control, lie to, manipulate, and steal from if they're depressed, dysfunctional, diseased, disoriented, disempowered, and in debt. I figured this out long ago. Something was and is very wrong with our society. Something wicked and evil this way comes. This evil force is now becoming brash, obvious, and walking above ground - since March of 2020. Some people on the planet are getting it worse than others, regarding how this structure sniffs out the innocent and then tries to actively snuff out all life's potential and beauty.

I feel for all of the defenseless humans, ones who are too weak or too small to defend themselves against this system. That feeling has never left me. I feel this way because I was one of those scared, vulnerable, and frightened kids in my youth. When I was young, I would often wonder why no one was protecting me and why no one would stand by my side to shield me from the dark forces in this world. I would often wonder what atrocity had to happen to me personally to get a mature adult guardian to rush to my side. That guardian never came and thus my spirit was forged in a blast furnace of fire, pain, heartache, and frustration. In the end, I made a pact with myself that if I were ever in the position where I could be the protector to others that I would follow through with that promise and spiritual contract.

Often great pressure can facilitate a transformation into something different, something better. I use my experience and hurl everything I have at the system, which has obviously abused billions before me. I am an Aries. I breathe fire. I write fire. I talk fire. The system is most likely getting back all it has given to me and more. I will never comply. I will never take a knee to this highly abusive, tyrannical, and corrupt machine that we call a "civilized society." This dark, rotting, and dirty system knocked me down but never broke the spirit that came with me to this planet. I, and millions like me, speak truth to power daily. As the famous Canadian Bruce Cockburn said, "You must kick at the darkness until it bleeds daylight." I'm not impressed with what's going on and I carry plenty of anger, but sometimes you can use the pain as a very powerful transformative fuel.

I've been writing and public speaking on a wide array of freedom-based issues for at least 20 years. People like myself saw the COVID-19 psychological operation gathering strength on the horizon for at least a decade. The control and energy extraction system of which I speak has a very simple design.

This system is comprised of two basic operations: indoctrination and poisoning. The indoctrination that's fired into our fertile minds comes primarily from government schooling, government policies, Hollywood movies, conventional radio, print media, and TV programs. This indoctrination and propaganda exist to program us to accept lies as truth. As social engineer Bertrand Russell once said, "The social psychologist of the future will have a number of classes of school children on whom they will try different methods of producing an unshakeable conviction that snow is black. When the technique has been perfected, every government that has been in charge of education for more than one generation will be able to control its subject securely without the need of armies or policemen."

When people believe that their vote counts, that the government exists to make their life better, that theft can be whitewashed using a label of taxation, that ingesting medical poison will improve health, or that working a meaningless and futile job is the best they can do, they've already been conditioned by these brainwashing systems to believe that snow is black.

If you think the media control of public perception through propaganda and indoctrination isn't bad enough, wait until you discover the other institutions waiting to ambush you and your family. Medicine, science, media, and government collude daily to drown the public in a never-ending tsunami of poisons that directly affect brain function, physical strength, and the spiritual courage needed for humans to operate as independent sovereign beings on this planet. This is the second cog in the machine of our collective enslavement: indoctrination first, poisoning second. The indoctrination is there to normalize, monetize, and incentivize the poisoning of the public. The right hand washes the left. Like any finely-tuned machine, the indoctrination hypnotically primes the public to act as their own worst enemy. The indoctrination is designed to have the public live out lies as truth. As you can easily observe today (and for decades prior), people in our communities can't stop hurting themselves with a non-stop barrage of poisonous assaults. This testifies to the power of our mind-control media system, which psychologically manipulates the public daily to self-abuse like it's an Olympic sport. What remains after this sleight of hand is a population too weak and too indoctrinated to resist their own enslavement.

You can't farm lions -- only lambs. This one-two punch of government/media indoctrination in conjunction with a never-ending tsunami of medical/science toxins combines to make the once-powerful human lion a very easily-ruled and domesticated lamb.

I've been speaking on these matters for decades. The COVID-19 psychological operation is simply an extension of a never-ending attack on the public. What the corrupt government, media, medical, and science systems are doing to the public now is merely a continuation of what they've always done. That's the problem in a nutshell.

So, what's the solution?

The solution is simple. You first need to develop the courage to process reality as reality. You need to step outside the mind-control based media and government system and take your power back. In order to do that, you need to know how brain-washing, mind control, and behavior modification operate. These are the methods by which you are programmed to believe that your vote counts or that injecting poison into yourself and your children will make them "better" or "healthier". This is how you are tricked into believing that working a job you don't like for 30 years is better than opening your own business and retiring in 10 years. This is how you are tricked into using your mouth as a garbage compactor and wasting most of your free time looking into a screen so you can repeat all the popular lies of the day in exchange for various infantile rewards of positive reinforcement. Brain-washing is how good people are tricked into conducting evil on this planet while still believing they are upstanding and moral citizens. Knowing how you are brainwashed and psychologically manipulated, by government and media, is very important if you want to unplug from this disempowering system of centralized control.

All brainwashing, mind control, and behavior modification run on a couple of basic principles. First, humans mimic what is repetitive in their environment. We all have a subconscious mind. The subconscious mind operates 24 hours per day, 365 days per year, without your conscious awareness. The subconscious controls 93-97% of your behavior. The subconscious has a job, and that job is to scan your environment, looking for what is repetitive. What is the most repetitive belief? What is the most repetitive thing to think? What is the most repetitive thing to say? What is the most repetitive behavior? The subconscious mind ranks and counts repetitive content, symbols, messages, products, services, and emotional imprints because the subconscious is in charge of our safety, security, and survival. The safety protocol designed into the subconscious mind is simple. The repetitive content represents what the bigger herd, wolf pack, or group is doing. There's more safety and security in the bigger group. Our survival depends on mimicking the repetitive content and taking up membership in the bigger herd.

Once the subconscious analyzes what the repetitive content of your environment is, it deems "what the majority is doing" as the safest card to play. After that, you simply act out that script and do your best to fit in. All humans believe that they're formulating their own behavior, but they're not. Humans copy, mimic, emulate, and mirror the most repetitive imprints or messages from their environment. This genetic survival mechanism worked great in our ancient past but what happens if the most repetitive messages in our environment today are purposely manufactured to be negative? Well, we copy those too. That's where the government and media corruption come into the picture.

To make a long story short, all your media and government policies are purposely manufactured to control the repetitive content absorbed into your subconscious. You become what you see on a repetitive basis. What's on the screen instantly appears on the street. Government and media drown you in negative, immoral, self-abusive, self-destructive, and unethical garbage content 24 hours per day. All on purpose. The government works together purposely with the media and drives evil, sadistic, and unhealthy content into your subconscious mind as their primary occupation. What follows is predictable and is what our social engineers count on. It's monkey see, monkey do. Anyone focusing on their TV, radio, or newspaper today will mimic this disastrous programming and destroy themselves while our human farmers giggle from behind the screen.

As we act out disastrous and satanic lives, it looks like we're doing it to ourselves. We believe we have chaotic existences because of bad luck, bad genes, or bad timing. That's why this media-driven behavior modification is so effective. We build our own worst lives, but the truth is that we're getting programmed to keep ourselves disempowered and messy while our social engineers work the puppet strings from behind the green curtain at Oz. We're all being programmed via documented behavior modification tactics to constantly dull our shine and to destroy our own innate human potential.

It doesn't matter what show or TV show is analyzed; we see all the same repetitive imprints: Caffeine consumption (coffee) is #1. Alcohol consumption is #2. General violence is #3. Violence/criminal conduct approved by or executed by government agencies is #4. Hyper-sexuality is #5. The single wine drinking female is #6. The weakened beta male, who lives inside a permanent childhood, is #7. Various forms of sexual confusion are #8. The hard-working factory laborer or person down on their luck, glorified as the most moral and noble, is #9. The independent successful businessperson is demonized -- that's #10. There are more, but our subconscious misses none of it and formulates our behavior from the repetitive content throughout all media. What we see is what we'll be. When these themes are repetitive throughout all media releases, our society is set to fall apart, as was always the design.

The people in the high bastions of power maintain their energy by destroying yours. Your government isn't what you think it is. The institutions that surround you aren't there to help you rise up into your full potential. Your TV shows and movies aren't there to entertain you. They're there to entrain you and throw you down the evolutionary ladder, back into a spiritual stone age. Humans need positive and uplifting repetitive content to be their absolute best. This is why everything outside of the media and government is perpetually negative and inverted. Strong and healthy societies can't be governed easily. Weak and unhealthy societies are easily dominated by the 1%.

We need you to come onto our team of empowered humans. It's time to turn off the TV and movies or at least recognize the never-ending stream of negative content they fire into your fertile subconscious. You need to surround yourself with positive, uplifting, and healthy repetitive content in order for you to manufacture positive, uplifting, and healthy behavior. We need to program our own behavior by controlling the repetitive content we take in through our eyes and ears.

Come join the truth to power movement. It's time. Take your life back. Adult up. Level up. Lion up. Let's bring morality and ethical conduct back to this planet. Let's plug into a better life. Build your dreams by taking full control of your behavior. A healthy and powerful society is made up of healthy and powerful individuals. I believe in you. Thank you for listening.

About Jason Christoff:

Jason Christoff is a self-sabotage expert who also runs an international self-sabotage coaching school. Jason discovered many years ago that manipulative psychology, behavior modification, brainwashing, mental conditioning, and mind control are continually weaponized against the public by media and government to make the public easier to control, govern, lie to, manipulate, coerce, and steal from. Jason's work is dedicated to exploring, discussing, exposing, and offering solutions to these modalities of covert public control.

You can contact Jason directly at jason@freedomfromselfsabotage.com to inquire about his education programs and school, which teach positive forms of brainwashing, so people can lead happier and more successful lives.

Chapter Eight

Love is My New Normal

By Alex Lasarev

Well, hello there! My name is Alex Lasarev.

My family escaped communism in The Soviet Union so I could be born free in Toronto, Ontario.

Now I've fled communism in Ontario so I could live semi-free in Vancouver, BC.

And if we lose the fight here, I'm moving to Florida.

I am a comedian, podcaster, conscious-preneur, and more.

I had a difficult upbringing. My mother was physically and psychologically abusive. My father left her when I was three. I ran away from home at 15, and my mother committed suicide when I was 18.

Because I never received the love I so desired from any parental figures - certainly not from my mother - I sought deeply to connect with women. I was extremely uncomfortable with rejection, and never approached members of the opposite sex. I tried following the advice of dating gurus within the somewhat shady "seduction community." This advice didn't help, and it was damaging to a degree because it emphasized non-authentic methods of connecting with women - mainly at nighttime with alcohol being a factor. This definitely wasn't my thing. Around 2006, I got the inspiration to try something radical. I decided I was going to simply approach women I found attractive - anywhere I ran into them. And I was going to be honest and tell them that I was interested in dating. I had quite some success with this and ended up coaching other men in how to do "Day game." This led to several viral videos and the explosion of an entire subculture of men running around the streets trying to pick up women. I ended up travelling around the world teaching these courses for many years. What I discovered during this period was that the number one thing that was holding men back from experiencing abundance with women was their fear of speaking their truth. Why? A deep fear of rejection. During my courses, I discovered that forcing me to directly face this fear was the fastest way to catapult them to success.

One very interesting pattern I'd noticed was that after the men overcame their fear of rejection with women, they would go on to make big changes in their lives. I realized that overcoming fear in one part of your life translated very quickly into other parts. It was a very fast jump from speaking their truth to living fearlessly. Some would quit their old thankless jobs. Some would let go of relationships. Some started the businesses they had always wanted. Some would move to different countries!

Many gifts show themselves when we stand in our truth. By speaking your truth, you will always attract the people with whom you really resonate, as well as drive away people with whom you don't. This is a great thing, because you end up only spending time with people who really love you for who you are - not for someone you're trying to be.

People fear losing friends, but ending relationships is a sign that you are growing. We cannot, nor are we supposed to, get along with everybody. We're supposed to REALLY get along and have deep relationships with our core tribe, but that tribe will not show up until YOU are REALLY showing up as who you are. If you are doing that, you will naturally push some people away from you. This is absolutely necessary. In fact, when you say NO to the things (and people) in your life that are not in alignment with who you are, you will attract the things and people that ARE in alignment. If you SETTLE for what you have, you are saying to the universe, "It's okay. This is good enough. I am not really worthy of more." And so it shall be because YOU are the creator of your reality. As soon as you DECIDE you want more out of life, and you actually take the ACTIONS required to bring in what you truly desire, then it will manifest. Until you clear the space by leaving the relationships (and circumstances) that are not in resonance, you couldn't have the time and energy to connect with your REAL tribe. The tribe that loves the real you. So embrace this change. Take action. Change is your best friend, if it comes out of your INTENTION!

My advice to all the beautiful humans out there trying to make a difference:

Do things that make you uncomfortable - on purpose.

Most people are stuck in life because they AVOID uncomfortable situations. You must become the opposite. You must learn to ENJOY uncomfortable situations. Then you will be unstoppable!

I know, it's a crazy concept. It's weird. It's awkward. But that's the point! Start small and build it up, and then one day you won't recognize yourself. When someone farts on a packed elevator (or there's a smell), tell everyone that you are the guilty one. Pick your nose aggressively when you're in a serious conversation with people. Bump into things and then fall over while people are watching. This stuff is super liberating and helps you not take life too seriously. It also builds up your social freedom muscles. It sounds crazy, but it will change your life. Just start small and look for opportunities to do and say things that are socially weird and awkward. Do it, have fun with it, and see what happens. Remember: The less you care what people think, the more you will speak your truth, and the more you will LIVE your life authentically. I've actually written a book that helps people with this.

Another small thing about speaking your truth is to always take a moment to check in with yourself: Take a deep breath, feel into your heart, and be SURE it is YOUR truth, then speak. Many people are just repeating other people's opinions. Do not be one of those people. Are you just speaking because you want to be heard? Or because you want to get the dopamine hit of "being right?" Or are you truly coming from a place of love and compassion? Are you sharing something because you actually want to help another being on their journey? That is the big question. Take a breath and FEEL into it. If it's not your truth, or you are angry, or you are unclear, the highest action is to remain silent until you are really ready. If you are overwhelmed by the idea of speaking your truth, start small. Start by saying "Yes" when you mean yes, and "NO!" when you mean no. Then build from there.

My next bit of advice, and probably the most important thing of all, at least in my humble opinion, is simply this: Find a way to contribute to this movement that truly resonates with you, and you do it! Interestingly, you can replace the words "this movement" with the word "life".

One of the most popular questions I've been asked over the years on my spiritual podcast is "How do I find my life's purpose?"

And the short answer is: keep doing things that you really love doing, and see where it leads you.

We're all here for our own unique spiritual journey, and we all have our own unique gifts. Some people came to the planet simply to witness this great awakening. Some people came here just to heal their trauma, so they could then help others. Some people came just to be an amazing mom or dad. If it feels right, it's probably right. What can you be doing in your life that's fun for you AND helps other people? Same thing goes for getting involved in the freedom movement. It's not about what you're doing, or measuring your "success" in doing it. It's about the energy and intention behind what you're doing. If you're investing energy into something that helps other people, that energy comes back at you in one form or another. That's universal law. When you do something you are truly passionate about, it raises your vibration. When you are in your joy, it raises other people up. WHAT you're doing isn't as important as how you are feeling when you're doing it. So get out there, and share your unique gift. It's what you came here for!

Never forget: The first part of speaking truth to power is being truthful to yourself. A wise man once said, "To betray another is bad. To betray yourself is infinitely worse."

Start within. Be true to yourself about where you are in life. About your needs, desires, habits. Be bold enough to stop deceiving yourself. From there you can speak your truth with others.

About Alex Lasarev:

Alex started stand-up comedy in 1997, because it was cheaper than therapy. From 2009 until 2015, he built a global cult following as a men's dating coach. Alex discovered that one's ability to attract amazing connections is in direct correlation to one's level of self-love and acceptance. In 2015, Alex founded the Infinite Man Summit, where he inspired thousands of men to live fearlessly.

Alex's spiritual awakening began in 2009. However, things moved very quickly from 2015. Alex travelled the world seeking enlightened masters and healers. In 2016, Alex started the *Woke As F**K Podcast*, where he interviews beings on the path of self-realization.

Alex is currently working on a comedy special, a conscious clothing line, and a number of other projects.

Alex's greatest passion is reminding everyone that their nature is love and that all we have to do to be happy is to start living our unique soul's purpose!

https://loveismynewnormal.com

Chapter Nine

My Journey to Truth and Power

By Ted Kuntz

My journey from parent to warrior began in earnest on December 16, 1984. That was the day my son Joshua experienced his first grand mal seizure.

Prior to this date, I was like most parents: I believed our governments were acting in our best interest. I believed our medical system was grounded in science and the ethic of informed consent. I believed our mainstream media was a source of unbiased information. And, pertinent to this conversation, I believed in the safety and effectiveness of vaccines to protect and improve the health of children and adults.

This belief was not based upon any personal research I did. Rather, it was based on my naïve trust in the goodness of government, my blind faith in the integrity of the medical profession, and the idea that I lived in a country where freedom of speech was the foundation of an independent media.

My Son, Joshua

My son, Joshua, was born in July 1984. His birth was unremarkable save he was three weeks overdue. Josh was a healthy and content baby. He suckled easily and was exclusively breastfed for the first six months. His mother and I remarked on how fortunate we were to have such a healthy baby.

When Joshua was four months of age, we dutifully took him to our family doctor for his first vaccination. There was no discussion of whether we would or would not consent to our son being exposed to this invasive medical treatment. It was a foregone conclusion. "Vaccines are safe and effective." "Vaccines save lives." "Every responsible parent vaccinates their child with every available Health Canada recommended vaccine." There was nothing to discuss.

Immediately following the injection, Josh became agitated. The doctor assured us that agitation is normal. However, the agitation persisted and increased in intensity. Something was not right with our once content and healthy child. Twice in the next two weeks we returned to the doctor to have him examine our ailing child. We were once again assured that there was nothing to worry about. In spite of the assurances, it was evident to his mother and me that the son we brought home from the doctor's office the day of the vaccination was not the same son we brought to the doctor's office.

On December 16, 1984, twenty-one days following his vaccine injection, Josh had his first seizure. It was a tonic seizure presenting as full body rigidity lasting approximately twenty-five minutes. Uncertain what was happening, we rushed him to the local hospital. Josh was prescribed anti-seizure medication and after an overnight stay he was discharged.

We were advised it was likely a febrile seizure. Not to be concerned. This sometimes happens following vaccination. The anti-seizure medication was simply a precaution.

Approximately one month later, Josh experienced a second seizure. This was a more aggressive tonic-clonic seizure with intense muscle contractions. The seizure lasted approximately twenty minutes. An ambulance was called and we returned to the same hospital. More tests, blood work, and scans, were administered to identify the cause of the seizures. All results came back as normal.

As a precaution, more anti-seizure medication was prescribed. The doctor, in his desire to be helpful, advised – *"Treat your son as a normal child and everything will be fine."* Unfortunately, everything wasn't fine. One month later, Josh seized again.

Josh continued to seize approximately every thirty days. Each seizure was a grueling fifteen to twenty minutes of intense convulsing. Eventually, the doctors at the local hospital advised us that Josh's condition was too complicated for their level of expertise. We were referred for more specialized care at Vancouver's Children's Hospital. Once there, a team of neurologists plied their skills and offered their therapies.

Over the next four years, Josh was prescribed numerous medications and combinations of medications, special diets, steroids, a maintenance dose of antibiotics, Valium, and not-yet-approved experimental drugs. Nothing worked. By the time Josh was three years of age, his delayed speech was evident. Shortly thereafter, Josh lost many of the developmental gains he had made – walking, talking, dressing himself, and feeding himself.

In spite of their best efforts, Josh's condition continued to deteriorate. The space between the seizures got shorter and shorter. By the time Josh was four years old, he was seizing twelve to fifteen times per day, with each seizure lasting fifteen to twenty minutes. In one three-month period, we called an ambulance more than thirty times.

When Josh was five years old, the chief neurologist took me aside. In a somber tone, he advised me to no longer bring my son to the hospital. He confided that there was nothing else they could do. He informed me that if my wife and I needed some respite from our son's condition, they would admit him to hospital, but they would no longer treat him.

Vaccine Injury?

Many times during my consultations with the doctors and specialists I put forward the question of whether my son had been adversely affected by his vaccine shot. I explained that Josh was born healthy and became ill following the injection.

The idea of my son's condition being related to the vaccine was immediately dismissed. Vaccines don't cause this kind of condition, I was told. Josh would probably have had a seizure disorder anyways, they reasoned. Vaccines are safe.

When I suggested they identify the manufacturer and lot number of the particular vaccine Josh received to ascertain whether other children reacted the way my son had, this request was denied. A waste of resources, I was told.

As I began to do more research into vaccine safety, I learned that many children had reacted to the DPT vaccine that Josh received; that neurological injuries, including an uncontrolled seizure disorder, were reported repeatedly in the medical literature. When I shared this information with the doctors, I was told this only happens in "one in a million" cases and it was unlikely Josh's condition was related to the vaccine. I was told that all this talk of vaccine injury was a waste of time and resources, as it wouldn't change how they medically treated my son. I simply needed to accept that my son was disabled.

When I requested that a report be filed with Health Canada to indicate the possibility that Josh had experienced an adverse reaction to the vaccine, I was told this wouldn't happen because I couldn't prove that Josh's condition was vaccine related. They acted as if it was my responsibility to prove vaccine injury. When I asked if they could prove that my son's condition wasn't vaccine related, they admitted that they couldn't.

When I persisted with my request of the family physician to have Josh's injury reported as a possible vaccine injury (the same physician who administered the shot), I was told that he would get "in trouble" if he filed a report claiming vaccine injury.

After the chief neurologist at Children's Hospital advised me not to bring my son back to the hospital, I began to pursue alternative health care options, including naturopathic and chiropractic care, acupuncture, chelation, homeopathic, and nutritional supplementation. These were all unfamiliar methods of treatment, but I had to try something to improve my son's condition. The naturopath immediately diagnosed vaccine injury.

In my effort to work collaboratively with both streams of medicine, I asked the naturopath to write a report of her findings. I explained that I wanted to share her assessment with the doctors at Children's Hospital. In spite of her reluctance, explaining that her findings would not be well received, I insisted. She forwarded a report to Children's Hospital.

Over the next three years, while under the care of the naturopath , Josh's condition improved dramatically. The seizures reduced in length from fifteen minutes to ten minutes, then seven, five, three, and eventually one minute. The frequency reduced from twelve to fifteen times per day to ten, five, one, every other day, and eventually to only four to six times per month.

On an annual basis we would arrange a consultation with the neurologists at Children's Hospital. They were very pleased with the improvement in Josh's seizure disorder. I asked if they would be interested in hearing what we were doing to improve his medical condition. They expressed interest. However, once I began to inform them of the treatments and remedies being provided by the naturopath, they immediately stopped me. They informed me they weren't interested in hearing such nonsense.

When I challenged them with the improvement they had witnessed in my son's condition, they responded, *"He likely would have gotten better anyways."* It was in moments like this that I came to recognize that these doctors were blinded by their allegiance to a medical paradigm and unable or unwilling to examine the medical evidence before them if it conflicted with their training and belief system.

When I asked if they received the report from the naturopath, they acknowledged that they had. The neurologist then informed me he *"put it where it belongs*". When I asked, *"Where?"* I was told, *"In the garbage."*

My Own Research

After my son's deteriorating health following the vaccine, I began to research for myself the scientific evidence for the claims of safety and efficacy. I gathered hundreds of research articles from the medical library at my local university. I wrote letters to the chief medical officer in my community requesting evidence of safety and effectiveness. He simply provided me with a photocopy of the introduction to a medical textbook describing vaccines as *"a miracle of modern medicine*". No scientific evidence of safety was ever provided.

I purchased as many books on the topic as I could find. Over a thirty-year period, I have accumulated a substantial library of articles, research papers, websites, blogs, books, and other information pertaining to vaccine safety and effectiveness.

Also, I met with hundreds of parents who shared with me similar stories of adverse events following vaccination.

I discovered that the mass vaccination of our children (and adults) is more complex and dangerous than we have been led to believe. I learned that the science is not settled. I learned that family physicians are largely uninformed about vaccine ingredients and the adverse effects of vaccines, and that they know even less about how to recognize and treat vaccine injury.

I learned that Canada is one of only two G20 nations without a vaccine injury compensation program. The other country is Russia.

I learned that the mainstream media has been captured by the financial richness of the medical/pharmaceutical industry and is unwilling to engage in open, thoughtful discussion about vaccines. Instead, there exists a 'de facto' blackout in the media that censors any information that acknowledges that vaccines can and do cause harm. This has been directly confirmed by journalists in the media.

I learned that vaccine manufacturers in the United States are not legally liable for the safety of their products, courtesy of an Act of Congress in 1986. And while no similar legislation of manufacturer immunity exists in Canada (excepting with the COVID injections), our courts have been unwilling to recognize and compensate victims of vaccine injury.

I learned that no government agency, medical professional, or public health official will take responsibility for the harm vaccines can and do cause. If your child is injured by a vaccine, you are on your own.

I learned that the DPT shot given to my son was eventually withdrawn from the North American market due to the significant number of neurological disorders attributed to the use of this product. This product, however, is still being used in third world countries because it is less expensive to produce than the replacement.

I have witnessed the medical industry's callous disregard for those who have experienced the harmful effects vaccines can and do cause. We are dismissed, discounted, disrespected, and silenced.

I learned that the vaccination program is essentially an uncontrolled experiment supported by exceptional marketing. There are no long-term studies that prove the current vaccine schedule is safe and effective. There are no long-term studies that prove vaccinated children have better overall health than unvaccinated children. In fact, the opposite is true. Studies conducted in the last few years clearly demonstrate that unvaccinated children are healthier and have fewer chronic health conditions than vaccinated children.

I learned that vaccines have not been tested for their ability to cause cancer (carcinogenicity), their ability to damage an organism (toxicity), their ability to damage genetic information within a cell (genotoxicity), their ability to change the genetic information of an organism (mutagenicity), or their ability to impair fertility.

I learned that the current vaccine schedule has never been tested for safety in the real-world way in which the schedule is implemented – giving multiple doses at once, or for long-term safety; that most vaccines on the market have been approved based on studies lasting only a few months or even weeks.

I learned that doctors receive no formal training on how to diagnose or treat vaccine injury. Instead, they learn how to convince "vaccine hesitant parents" to accept the vaccination of their children.

I learned that the calls for mandatory vaccination violate medical law, which enshrines the individual's right to voluntary, informed consent to medical risk-taking as a foundational medical ethic.

I learned that coercive vaccination also violates:

- The Canadian Charter of Rights and Freedoms, including the guaranteed freedoms of conscience and religion, and the legal right to security of the person.
- International conventions, including the Nuremberg Code and Helsinki Accords, defend the basic human right to the informed consent ethic and reject the moral argument that the creation of alleged benefits for the many justify the sacrifice of the few.
- The Universal Declaration on Bioethics and Human Rights; Article 6 – Consent: "*Any preventive, diagnostic and therapeutic medical intervention is only to be carried out with the prior, free and informed consent of the person concerned, based on adequate information. The consent should, where appropriate, be expressed and may be withdrawn by the person concerned at any time and for any reason without disadvantage or prejudice.*"

I came to the realization that I was not given any information by the medical industry to ensure I was giving informed consent to the medical procedure of vaccinations. Given the above, I reached the conclusion that the medical industry is more invested in protecting the vaccine market than in protecting the health of our children.

COVID-19 - Pandemic or Fraud?

Thus, when COVID-19 presented to the world in March 2020, I already had a healthy skepticism for the claims of our governments, public health, and mainstream media. I wondered if we truly were in the grip of a world-wide pandemic or in the tyranny of a manufactured crisis. When the two weeks to “flatten the curve” become “there is no return to normal until we have a vaccine and every human is injected”, I knew we were in the throes of a global pandemic of fraud.

What was labeled as ‘conspiracy theory’ in July 2020 has become the declared agenda of the World Economic Forum, GAVI, the CDC, and the World Health Organization. The medical ethic of informed consent, the foundational principles of the scientific method, and the principles and values of our Charter of Rights and Freedoms have been sacrificed at the altar of a “global emergency.”

I now recognize that my entire life has prepared me to be a warrior for truth. My efforts to understand the disabling of my beautiful son by our medical system, my experience of the callous disregard for the harm caused, and my futile efforts to bring truth to the masses via engagement with our elected representatives and mainstream media have prepared me with the gift of sight.

I can see what so many are unwilling or unable to see: that systemic deception, distortion, manipulation, and corruption have hollowed out the fundamental structures of a free and just society.

I hold the perspective that this is not the 'Great Reset' as proposed by Klaus Schwab, Executive Chairman of the World Economic Forum, but rather the 'Great Reveal'. The darkness that has captured humanity for decades, possibly forever, is finally being made known.

I believe that this is the time of humanity's awakening. This is the time of our transformation. This is the time to claim our power and our authority as divinely created beings who have an inherent right to freedom due to our Creator, and not as a consequence of the benevolence of our governments.

I believe the rising of humanity has just begun. This time of suffering has awakened and galvanized freedom warriors globally to rise up and claim what is rightfully ours.

This will not be an easy battle. The forces against us are very powerful. But they do not have the power of truth behind them. These forces are not life-giving, but rather life-ending. Their destruction is not in doubt. However, in order to end this evil agenda, humanity needs to rise up and claim its authority.

I honour those who walk this path and who are willing to sacrifice everything to safeguard the rights and freedoms that are inherently ours. I am in gratitude to those who rise above the deception and hold true to their integrity. And I honour my son and the journey that we walked together. I was strengthened by the struggles and gifted with hard-earned wisdom.

I feel privileged to be serving humanity in this way at this time. There is nothing more important, and I serve with gratitude and faith in a better world.

Ted Kuntz

About Ted Kuntz:

Ted Kuntz is a father and grandfather, a medical choice activist, author, and educator. Kuntz's journey to examine the claims of the vaccine industry began after his son Joshua was neurologically injured by the diphtheria-pertussis-tetanus vaccine (DPT) in 1984.

Kuntz began a journey to understand what happened to his son. This journey revealed that the medical industry has been systematically and intentionally dishonest with health consumers on the safety, effectiveness, and necessity of vaccinations.

Kuntz believes the organized and intentional effort to deny citizens their right to make medical decisions for themselves and their children is one of the greatest threats to humanity today.

If we lose the capacity for choice over what is injected into our self and our children, then we are no longer free citizens. Protecting medical choice and demanding honesty, transparency, and accountability are the most important issues in Kuntz's life today.

Ted Kuntz is a retired psychotherapist and the author of a number of books including: *Peace Begins With Me; How Can I Wake Up When I Don't Know I'm Asleep*?; and *Dare to Question – One Parent to Another.*

Kuntz is the current President of Vaccine Choice Canada.

Kuntz's son Josh passed away in February 2017 after a life of uncontrolled seizures and diminished capacity due to vaccine-induced neurological injury.

Chapter Ten

How They Remember You

By Marcella Desjarlais

As a child, I grew up as a crown ward. I was bounced from foster home to foster home; a survivor of the 60's scoop. In my childhood, I endured racism as well as all manner of abuse. None of these things have kept me down in the throes of addiction or wallowing in my regret from poor choices I had made. Instead, they have helped me grow, taught me many lessons, and made me strive to be a better person. I became someone who contributed positively to society. I became someone who can empathize and relate to others from all walks of life. I live every day aspiring to inspire and assist others along their life journeys.

My educational and employment background spans many sectors. I am a graduate with a Bachelor of Business Administration with a major in Marketing. I was also my class valedictorian. My career history has involved working in real estate as a realtor and managing broker (13 years), a team assistant for the provincial government, and a Health Administrative Assistant and Administrative Assistant to the CEO of two different non-profit organizations dealing with health for Indigenous people. Currently, I am working as the Ombudsperson for my alma mater, part-time for a temp agency doing administrative work, and I occasionally take house-cleaning jobs for an amazing company owned by freedom fighters. I am a Jackie-of-all-trades.

Prior to 2020, I was living life to the fullest. In anything that involved friends, family, travel, church, food, and fun times, I was there! I have always been one to share my story of hardship in the hopes of helping others feel the same fire and passion that I have burning inside me.

Speaking truth to power is taking my life experiences and showing others that although we endure hardships, struggles, and grief, truth can transform tribulations into power that propels us forward to whatever our visions of success are. We can turn the negatives into fuel to drive us. It is getting up, enduring everything the day throws at you, and engaging in meaningful activities and conversation that spreads hope to others.

During the early days of the "pandemic", I tuned in daily at 3 PM to hear the latest numbers (due to the workplace I was at) with the rest of my teammates. About two weeks in, I could not listen to the "droney" voice of Bonnie and started to have an inclination that things were not right. As a follower of Christ, I began to see similarities in current events that fit Biblical scripture. I decided then to turn those mind-numbing daily reports off. Instead, I started listening to a friend who was showing credible messages and legitimate information. I guess you could say that was my awakening to the forever-unfolding saga we see in the world today: a desire to share truths to help strengthen friends, family, and communities; an opportunity to bring information to assist in their decision-making for the best outcomes for their health and safety – for them, and by them.

This friend was starting a protest group in my local city, Surrey, and asked if I wanted to attend. Without hesitation, I confirmed "I would be all in." I assisted with the group flyers of every event (clear across the country) and was admin on the Facebook group. My first speech was on July 1, 2020, in Victoria, BC. I shared my workplace story of my time on the

Occupational Health and Safety Committee and the masking mandates coming down.

Shortly after that, in July, I joined Hugs Over Masks (HOM). At the time of this writing, I am the managing director. It started with seeing the T-shirt. I wanted one. After speaking with the founder of HOM, Vlad, we decided to branch off from Ontario and bring the first group, led by me, to BC. Our first rally was in August, at Holland Park in Surrey, with about 50 people. The media arrived and I declined an invitation to speak. We were already starting to see the "anti" prepositions to anything for which we were standing, and their one-sided derailing agenda.

Since July 1, 2020, many things have happened:

- I have spoken at each freedom rally and weekly protest held at the Vancouver Art Gallery (VAG).
- HOM moved from Surrey to Kitsilano beach in Vancouver. Then, in the fall, it moved to the VAG, where we shared rallies with The Liberty Club (run by my friend Danna) and No New Normal (run by my friend Raoul).
- Our three groups traveled to Vancouver Island and Kelowna to support and host many rallies, and we organized rallies and speakers who had credible information to share on various topics dealing with masks, vaccines, financial crisis, small businesses, and, of course, freedom.

As time has passed, I have found my God-given voice growing more passionate about current events affecting all of us, and a boldness to share from my heart. At this time, COVID vaccines are the hot topic. I have been around mRNA-vaccinated individuals and I can report that I, my grandchildren, and my oldest child have first-hand experience dealing with shedding/ transmission of vaccine spike proteins. This is one of those instances that compel me to speak at these rallies -- to share my truths in hopes it might help families make more informed decisions on health matters instead of just taking what the government or media reports say. An individual's testimony is powerful.

I have followed many doctors online and locally. At the moment, I have connections with a trauma psychologist, my family doctor, a natural medicine practitioner, and a clinical counsellor. As well, I have followed people, such as Dr. Tenpenny, Dr. Kulwinder Kaur, and Vaccine Choice Canada. Also, I research and look for credible sources that are confirmable with data. If the media or government says something, I'm going out there to search for deeper insight. As the Bible says to work out your own salvation, likewise I'm going to seek out my own information.

Knowing who to trust and who not to trust or believe is tenuous at best. Government doctors and health professionals wrapped up in the agenda of COVID are people I generally do not believe. They have not provided us with anything that would help us get healthy, nor do they provide the actual data to citizens to ease their fears. Instead, they push vaccines and implement disastrous "safety" plans that have caused massive collateral damage, such as bankruptcy for small business owners and massive increases in drug overdoses and suicides. There is a looming mental health crisis for everyone, including young children, that is being ignored so the exaggerated COVID measures can continue unabated.

As the COVID narrative carried on through 2020, I lost friends and blocked others who were not of the same mindset and found that I was too aggressive with my Facebook posts of counter-government narrative. For the most part, my immediate family is in the same mindset as me. In the summer of 2020, I took sick leave from work and attended counselling through my employer as a member of a health team. My stress level was going up due to the nature of my work. I resigned in the fall, as I could not push out work to the citizens we served when it went against my conscience.

My soul has been laid bare online with everything I have shared. At times, I have shared some very personal information. Occasionally, I felt I had shared too much, until I heard from people thanking me, that it encouraged or motivated them. Other times I have shared me just being me. Being me sometimes means being silly and simply enjoying life, and at times it means being serious, caring, and informative. Other than not shopping at the malls anymore, I have not changed my lifestyle. I do what I have always done: live life to the fullest.

My predominant modes of communication are Facebook; Telegram, for planning and organizing events and rallies; and Zoom meetings, texting, and telephone calls with my circle of friends.

Discernment is difficult for me. Sometimes I second guess myself. For the most part, everyone gets the benefit of the doubt and respect from me. There are many I hold at arm's length because I question their authenticity. I have been correct on more than one occasion, so it's always best for people to trust their gut feelings -- to observe, listen, and then respond.

As a Bible-believing church girl, I share verses that are uplifting and empowering -- things that will help take the focus off the fear and put it onto positive thoughts and actions. Fear paralyzes the soul and having a sound mind and heart of genuine love releases that fear. As much as I am asked and invited to, I always support and lift others up with ideas and things they can do to reach their goals and be better. Sometimes it's just being that listening ear, singing a song, or having a good laugh together that moves them from one situation to the next in a positive way.

My main message is to stand up and speak out. Do not be silent. Silence does not help others act. I have participated in leadership roles and training over the years. As a Marketing major, I learned different styles of presentations. I am excellent at persuasive speeches with a call to action. This is my style and I feel it can be used with every topic that will help others to rise and fight.

What is the best advice that I can give others with regards to speaking truth to power? You can sit, stay silent, and let things happen around you, or you can stand up and act to create beneficial change. That one choice, although seemingly small, produces ripples that can perpetuate change! Action and inaction both have consequences: positive and negative, short-term and long-term. The choice belongs to you alone. It is your legacy.

"You are always only one choice away from changing your life." ~ Mac Anderson

About Marcella Desjarlais:

As a First Nations mother to three amazing daughters and grandmother to four beautiful grandchildren, Marcella is determined to set fire to the past and burn a new path towards a glorious future, not only for her family but for ALL Canadians.

Marcella grew up predominantly in the Lower Mainland, graduating from college with a BBA with a Marketing Major. She has worked for the provincial government and various organizations that assist First Nations and Metis citizens. She has also been in the real estate industry for 13 years and counting.

Since April of 2020, Marcella has been a freedom fighter, speaking at protests and freedom rallies.

As a candidate and a proud member of the PPC, Marcella is looking forward to having the opportunity to confidently represent her constituents in parliament. With listening and hard work, she believes she has the ability to ensure Canada has thriving communities, supported small businesses, and a booming economy. Marcella is willing to do whatever it takes. She is here to serve the people who value their rights and the freedoms for which young men and women fought and died. She stands for the values upon which our beloved country was founded.

Chapter Eleven

The Liberti Club

By Danna Bresciani

Right from the get-go, I wasn't an easy child. I danced to a different tune. As soon as I was born, I was tough as nails. The medical staff had to put me in an incubator because I wasn't displaying the usual signs (I wouldn't cry). Maybe that moment in time was the best for my parents. "It was the calm before the storm."

Being the middle child, I never really felt that I fit in. Looking back, I don't think I was content with the role because I think I knew somehow that I was here for something much larger and greater.

I spent a lot of time trying to get attention because I didn't feel I was being heard the way I needed to be. I think it's because I was what they call "a spirited child". I was intuitive but never understood what really was happening when I was young. I could feel all the energy of the people in a room and was largely affected by it. I didn't know how to turn it off, so I took it on. This made me act out. I was frustrated a lot, had many temper tantrums, and I couldn't understand why nobody understood me. I remember having a temper tantrum so bad when I was about two years old that I literally pulled out all the drawers of my dresser and banged my head on the floor until my head was black and blue. My poor mother.

Growing up, I was very blessed. As a child, I spent a lot of time out in nature and, looking back, I was very connected to it. We often would go on family trips that involved the outdoors, like camping, boating, fishing, and skiing.

Life when I was young was very different than it is for the kids growing up today. Nowadays, the connection to nature is fading because of the distractions of technology and social media, which I find incredibly sad.

As a teenager, I joined Air Cadets, went on bush camps, was in a marching band, and was also on the drill team. Somehow, I still beat my own drum, even in the pre-military. I'd often have to do push-ups for breaking the rules because I wanted to wear makeup "secretly". I kept getting caught though. Thankfully, the commanding officer of our squadron had a penchant for fun!

Shortly after this point, my life took a very different turn. I was in a serious car accident as a passenger. The car rolled and flipped end-over-end, landing upright. That changed me forever. It was a near death experience for one, but also, somehow, I knew in advance that this was going to happen -- so much so that I made the driver pull over and put on his seat belt prior to driving on this particular road, which ended up saving his life. This trauma caused a great deal of anxiety for me, but it was suppressed until about four years after the accident. To this day, no one really knows how I was able to get out of the car after I became conscious. Also, there was a massive propane tank in the vehicle that should have exploded but miraculously it never did. Why?

Life is a journey. Most importantly, we are here to learn about "Who We Are". We have all had experiences in our lives, both negative and positive, that have impacted us on a personal level. It is a choice where we let it take us.

The one thing I have come to recognize is that we are all seeking something. But what?

We've been looking and searching for something that fulfills our own voids. It is a part of finding out who we are.

It's my personal belief that we need to look inside ourselves but facing who we are is not an easy task. It means realizing that we all have faults and we need to step outside of our own egos to figure things out.

I've had many people over the years tell me "you're so deep". What does that even mean? Maybe I am? I thought I was just being normal. Maybe I am different? Or maybe I've just been trying to figure out this game called life?

I always felt there was more to what I was seeing on the surface and that is part of how I awakened to the corruption in the world and the driving forces behind it. What's happening in this world, and why? I never grew up in organized religion, but even without formal teachings I knew in my heart there was something divine guiding me. I could feel it even as a young child.

Looking back, I had premonitions about things to come that started back in 1994, but I would say I wasn't formally awakened until 2012, which I call my activation date. The reason I call it that is because everything started to come undone for me and I couldn't get it back together.

I've often heard that once you've been red-pilled, or "awakened", you can't go back.

The disruption and strain on my family life and marriage were unsettling. Partially due to my beliefs and ideas, however, I also felt an unseen driving force behind what I was experiencing and seeing, so I chose to continue down the rabbit hole I was in. It proved to be a LOT more difficult than I imagined.

I knew there was something wrong, so I started to look deeper and outside of the mainstream. I was shocked to discover that much of the things that were changing have been going on for quite some time.

I began to pay attention to the diversionary tactics, manipulation, and propaganda. They call it a TV "program" for a reason.

I felt alone in my journey, misunderstood, angry at what I was learning, frustrated, and just overall sad. Everything upon which I had built my life, from what we were told, was all a lie. I noticed the brainwashing and indoctrination everywhere. It isn't hard if you have eyes to see and ears to hear. You just need to pay attention. Unfortunately, there weren't a lot of resources to find this stuff when I started out, and I was constantly looking for and listening to different independent media, as well as paying attention to things in real time. I noticed that people aren't well-liked when they try to speak up because I was always getting into heated situations when trying to express what I knew.

"No one is hated more than he who speaks the truth" - Plato

In June of 2018 I was drugged and kidnapped. It's so strange because I never thought something like that could happen to me. I was tough as nails, remember? I won't go into too many details of that event; however, I can say that I know for certain the only reason I'm here today was because of divine intervention. I never got justice, though.

Not getting justice played an integral role in where I am today and why I ended up on the path I'm on. I thought I had my own plan mapped out for me. I guess God had a different one in mind.

When COVID-19 mysteriously made its way out into the mainstream media, I was already well aware that the world was not going in a positive direction. Initially, I was a bit concerned about the virus, but as time went on, I realized something more sinister was at play. Critically looking at the situation and who the players involved in the crisis were, I felt strongly that there was a hidden agenda behind what we were all being force-fed by the mainstream media and our governments. Why was Event 201, a "pandemic simulation event", performed not long before COVID-19? How come the sale of PCR tests started well before the actual crisis? Why was everything so controlled, with the same talking points and terms being used all around the world? There are no coincidences.

"Blind Belief in authority is the greatest
enemy of truth" – Albert Einstein

Being on lockdown helped me to reflect. During this time, I'd go on walks and ask God, "What is it I'm supposed to do?"

I felt so strongly that something needed to be done to help the public understand that there was another side to what we were all experiencing. Shortly after this moment, my mother alerted me to a protest not too far from us in North Surrey. It was at this protest that seeds started to grow in my mind. I instantly started to use my creative abilities so I could help in any way I could. I used my marketing skills to try to help bring attention to the group in hopes we would gain more traction. It started to work!

That being said, soon after our successes, problems began to develop. Nothing is easy. I quickly realized that as much as there is a positive spiritual force pushing you forward, there is also a spiritual component that is not positive trying to undermine success.

By this point, I was about three months into my investment in this group, but I was quickly realizing that not all parties involved were on the same page. I started to lose hope and everything I put into it was about to fail. I decided to leave the group I was trying to help.

Thankfully, Susan Standfield, another freedom fighter and activist with wisdom and experience, gave me some excellent advice and encouragement. Without her encouragement and moral support, I may have stepped out completely. This was a huge turning point for me. It was almost like a spiritual guide giving me a bit of a push.

I took a bit of time to reflect upon what Susan said to me, and a much-needed week off. I decided to reinvent and re-emerge. So, I founded The Liberty Club.

The Liberty Club is very special to me. I wanted it to be different and I wanted it to be built with strong roots out of my love for God and the human family. The acronym of TLC has a few meanings built into it, aside from the name itself:

The first is Tender Loving Care. I believe everything needs to start from a place of love.

Secondly, it means The Last Chance. We have reached a very critical time in human history, especially with the advancements in technology and the emergence of AI. It's so important to come together as a collective and to help awaken those still unaware of what we're facing. If we want to secure a future of freedom and unlimited human potential, it can only happen once the masses awaken to the horrors that have kept mankind in a constant state of slavery and bondage. The current system has been designed and inflicted upon us intentionally to inhibit our true purpose and potential. It takes brave souls with the same love for humanity to step forward and nudge the sleeping out of their trance.

There is much persecution for those trying to get the truth out, but I truly believe the Bible verse that says: "For nothing is secret, that shall not be made manifest; neither any thing hid, that shall not be known and come abroad. – Luke 8:17

My mission for The Liberty Club was to help bring this evil to the surface. This is why I built TLC. Part of my goal was to design a web page that would act as a resource center for upcoming events, but also to help newly awakened people to navigate information easier than it was for me in the past. So, I worked hard and created TheLibertyClub.ca.

Another goal I had was to connect with people on a personal level. My strategy was a bit unique, but I felt that if I brought food it would help to build trust for people inquiring about TLC. I also wanted the existing freedom warriors to be able to enjoy their experience and have fun.

My mother has been a large part of TLC because her passion for freedom and her talents have proven to be very helpful to me. People love to talk to her and she really is young at heart. Thanks for being there for me, Mom!

TLC merchandise was designed to help get thought-provoking messages out to the public. I feel it's important for people to come to their own conclusions and discernment, but a little push to help people use their brains in a different way is necessary, in my opinion. Every little bit helps.

I've never had any expectations as to where TLC will end up. The last thing I want is for any type of ego to lead me down the wrong path. I prefer divine guidance. This time is so much greater and my role is just another part of a bigger picture. I'm very protective of The Liberty Club because I want it to be remembered as being something beautiful. I am hoping that one day it will go through a different kind of transformation: one of healing.

There are so many blessings that come out of this kind of work. I've met some of the most generous and loving people. The true rewards and blessings have been given through acts of kindness and gratefulness that have been bestowed upon me by those souls around me. So many people have thanked me for what I am doing and there is nothing greater than that. To see the smiles and the love from all the people makes everything worthwhile and wonderful. God and the people inspire me in moving forward. It's their love, the love of God, and my love for them that keeps me going.

About Danna Bresciani:

Danna moved to British Columbia from Edmonton, Alberta when she was about two years old. As a child, she was very spirited, but as time went on, she refocused her energies on her creative abilities. Danna has done interior decoration for many events such as weddings, birthday parties, and baby showers over the years. Her passion for interior decorating has been a real focus of enjoyment for her. Prior to founding The Liberty Club, Danna worked in the dental industry, managing many offices as well as study clubs. Danna is a mother of two and loves children. She often spends time with family and close friends. She loves nature and all of the beauty it has to offer. She is a humanitarian and truth seeker. She hopes that one day humanity will discover its hidden mysteries and be able to enjoy true freedom, peace, and unlimited potential.

TheLibertyClub.ca

Twitter: @Dannab1

Chapter Twelve

Breaking Ranks

By Police On Guard For Thee

Police on Guard was formed in December of 2020, but many of us feel as though we have been a part of this organization since before its inception. A common theme when speaking to members is that they are often the outliers within their services. They are and always have been the officer with an opinion, the officer who speaks out, and the officer who is willing to take a stand for what they believe in. Police on Guard have always been there, within these individual members and their ideals across this great nation, only now have we come together as one voice. Although I am writing this from my perspective as just one member of the group, I hope that the following words echo the sentiments of all members.

Policing is a unique career. It is complex, difficult to describe, and even more difficult to understand. Being an officer should be a calling -- a calling to help people, to exude the values of our democracy, and to honour our oath to the constitution. As complex a career as policing is, it can be broken down into a simple question, from a moral, ethical, and legal perspective: What is the right thing to do in any given situation? Unfortunately, this is not the only question by which police services operate. Within the organizational structure, there are political and personal motivations that often cause the aforementioned altruistic approach to become blurred. When the interests of an individual override their lawful duties, the system breaks down and erodes the public trust in police.

Sir Robert Peel said, "The police are the public and the public are the police."

So, how did our organization start? In December of 2020, Canada was about nine months into the declared COVID-19 pandemic. While public health orders varied from province to province, it was evident that the public policy approach increasingly infringed on the guaranteed rights of Canadian citizens.

Police on Guard for Thee was instituted by several active and retired officers. We published an open letter on social media calling on various stakeholders to give clear and concise direction to the men and women of law enforcement. This letter was written in response to the arrest of a Calgary man who was playing hockey on an outdoor rink with his friends and family. This incident brought to the forefront the illogical nature of the public health measures surrounding COVID-19. We also saw arrests that were made for protesting, for not wearing masks, and for participating in religious gatherings. Police repeatedly entered private residences without a warrant and criminalized peaceful assembly, which is utterly unacceptable. These incidents, along with the outright government propaganda discouraging law-abiding citizens from exercising their basic human rights, catalyzed the launch of our organization. We needed to bring forth an alternate message: We, as active police officers, did not agree with what was happening across our country.

Immediately following the formation of our organization, we received widespread public support. As active officers, we were in a difficult position, since the Police Services Act prohibits us from speaking publicly on issues related to our duties. For this reason, we focused on honouring the service of our retired members and featuring their profiles on social media. This approach helped legitimize and grow our organization.

There's an old adage, "once a cop, always a cop." In speaking with retirees across the country, this was abundantly clear. Every member with whom we spoke echoed the same sentiments. They expressed that the public's trust in police was deteriorating, that police were acting unlawfully and unconstitutionally, and that they wished they were still on the job so they could do something about it. One of the most rewarding parts of this movement is that retired officers have been given a voice.

While our group began in Ontario, it quickly expanded to other provinces. Additional open letters were published by active law enforcement officers in Nova Scotia and Alberta. Retired officers pledged their support to our movement. Len Faul, a retired Toronto Police Inspector with 42 years of policing experience, reached out to us and later became our spokesperson. Law enforcement from other countries, including Denmark, the United States, the United Kingdom, and Australia have contacted us via email to join our membership. Men and women of the Canadian Armed Forces also felt strongly about our mission statement and are now counted in our numbers, along with members from Correctional Services, the Canada Border Services Agency, and Fire Services. Civilians have also graciously volunteered their time to assist our organization by lending their unique skill sets and perspectives.

As our numbers continue to grow, we have transitioned our group into a not-for-profit organization. Retired RCMP officers Clay Farnsworth and Wendy Long serve as our President and Secretary. Bert Mayo serves as our Treasurer, and Retired Fire Chief, William Clark, serves as one of our directors. William is also a talented singer-songwriter. He wrote and performed our Police on Guard anthem entitled *We Are Canadian*, which is available on iTunes. The following also serve as directors of our organization: Chris Vandenbos, Matt Silver, Rob Stocki, Terri Hayder, Angie Scott, Brittany Grenci, and Matthew Blacklaws.

What started as a movement by police officers now includes Canadians from every walk of life. The feedback that we have received from the public has been overwhelming. Whether via social media or in person at rallies and protests, common themes of thanks, gratitude, and hope are often expressed. Many Canadians also reach out to offer help and support in any way they can.

We all see the harmful effects of current policies, whether it's declining mental health, suicides, overdoses, increased alcohol use, domestic violence, child abuse, economic decline, the division within society, or the toxic culture of fear. As police officers, it's our job to look at the totality of any situation and act within a lawful, moral, and ethical framework. The focus of our organization has always been on the lawfulness of public health orders. We have read through all the applicable legislation and provide information to both the public and the police to support our position that provincial legislation does not supersede the individual liberties guaranteed by the Charter of Rights and Freedoms.

Perhaps the most important development in Police on Guard's timeline is when leading constitutional lawyer, Rocco Galati, of the Constitutional Rights Centre, agreed to represent nineteen active and retired Ontario police officers in a statement of claim filed with the Ontario Superior Court in May of 2021. Many of those officers are members of Police on

Guard. While what they have risked is not inconsequential, it is not the primary measure of their oath and their duty.

As Peter Drucker said, "What you have to do and the way you have to do it is incredibly simple. Whether you are willing to do it is another matter."

To paraphrase the above quote, "It's easy to do the hard thing when it's the right thing to do."

Active officers from the Toronto Police Service, York Regional Police Service, and Hamilton Police Service were named as applicants, along with retired members of the RCMP, Ottawa Police Service, and the Niagara Regional Police Service. Additionally, several applicants remained anonymous for fear of reprisals from their employers. To our knowledge, this is the first time in Canadian history that active and retired officers have filed a court action against their government. The respondents in this court action are the Attorney General for Ontario, Premier Doug Ford, Her Majesty The Queen in Right of Canada, James Ramer (Chief of Police, Toronto Police Service), Jim Mac Sween (Chief of Police, York Regional Police), Bryan MacCulloch (Chief of Police, Niagara Regional Police), Peter Sloly (Chief of Police, Ottawa Police Service), Eric Girt (Chief of Police, Hamilton Police Service), and the Attorney General of Canada.

To speak to what each individual has risked by taking this step would be difficult. In general terms, the applicants have risked their reputations and, in the case of the active officers, their careers. COVID is such a divisive issue that questioning or voicing opinions that oppose the mainstream narrative get many labeled as anti-maskers, anti-vaxxers, and spreaders of misinformation. Why do these terms have such negative connotations? Although Police on Guard does not take a position on these particular issues, we do take a stand when it comes to the constitutionality of these measures and an individual's right to choose as guaranteed by the Charter. These extreme labels are used to deflect from the actual issues at hand and discredit organizations and individuals who advocate for our rights when it comes to these matters. When the truth that we speak opposes the narrative that so many believe, we are categorized in a way that discourages others from supporting us. This includes family, friends, and coworkers.

Another question we often hear is why are some officers silent? To answer this, it's important to understand the police culture. Officers, and first responders in general, deal with incredibly difficult and often traumatic situations daily. In the context of current public health measures, while many officers may disagree with, or even realize that the orders are unlawful and unconstitutional, they remain neutral. This seems illogical to many, but when exposed to frequent and continued trauma, this response is a built-in coping mechanism. The pandemic is seen as just another shitty radio call that you need to get through to survive, to go home to your family, to salvage some semblance of normalcy. The difference is that this call has been going on for two years now. The difference is that when complaints about conduct, lawsuits, and possibly even criminal charges are filed, no excuse will suffice. This is another reason why we are doing what we are doing.

There is a culture within law enforcement that is inherently protective of our own. We know that some officers are struggling. The gamut of complications common amongst police is staggering: domestic issues, substance abuse, mental health, work stress, PTSD, etc. While it's our job to know legislation, we can see how many are just trying to get through their day-to-day lives. For this reason, Police on Guard has also become a quasi support network, a safe place for officers who are struggling, who need somewhere to turn.

Since mainstream media seems to only report the government's position on current events while ignoring, or referring with vitriol to, any information challenging their narrative, Police on Guard primarily uses social media to spread our message. Since this channel is not immune to censorship, we also launched a website where people can subscribe to our newsletters and see alternative content like podcasts. We even arrange to have members attend protests where they can speak to the masses and meet people face to face. While these avenues are helpful and effective, their reach is not nearly as vast as mainstream sources.

Thankfully, members of our group possess a variety of skill sets that are used collectively to help us reach our desired goals. We have some talented public speakers, tech-savvy persons, some who could be considered savants with various aspects of interpreting law and others who are very gifted in speaking with people and building in-person relationships. All of these strengths come together and work as one to keep the machine running.

Early in their careers, police officers become effectively experienced at collecting and analyzing information. Officers use the information they gather to paint a picture of a certain circumstance and then use discernment to decide on a course of action. We are no strangers to public scrutiny and are quite versed in presenting information to people who have opposing beliefs or preconceived notions about a situation. Unfortunately, we are still at a point in history where presenting an alternative viewpoint can result in attacks, modern-day witch hunts, and all-out character assassinations.

As previously mentioned, there is a plethora of labels used to discredit anyone expressing an unpopular opinion. These terms often require no proof to support their use and simply need to be stated by someone with credentials and confidence to dismiss those at whom they are directed. As the Danish writer/philosopher, Soren Kierkegaard, once said, "once you label me, you negate me." Call someone a name and what they have to say loses validity.

With all these tactics used to cast doubt, how does one discern fact from fiction?

This is not easy to answer. The ability to judge information, break it down, analyze, and think critically are not inherited virtues, at least not in the opinion of this seasoned officer. One could argue that building this skill requires a few core building blocks.

Firstly, keep an open mind. If you limit the scope of what you accept to be true using only the confines of your personal beliefs, you are doing yourself a disservice. Too often, we reject that which we do not understand or what seems absurd upon first glance. This is commonly referred to as cognitive dissonance, a term used to indicate the mental conflict that occurs when strongly held beliefs are contradicted or challenged with new information. Unfortunately, the common response is to dismiss new information in order to preserve a belief system. Far too many people lack an open mind nowadays and, as a result, they are trapped within a self-imposed prison of limited enlightenment. This stops them from acquiring new skills and tools which could be useful in understanding the world around them. This does not apply solely to our current pandemic but to all aspects of the human experience.

Secondly, it's important to understand that the first narrative presented isn't always an accurate one. Many situations are fluid and subject to change with the receipt of new information and/or clarification of the old. Any experienced police officer will tell you that it is very rare that the initial details you were provided about a situation are completely accurate. After further evidence-gathering and assessment of the situation, the facts often reveal themselves. We cannot commit ourselves to blindly accepting the message delivered with the ringing of the first bell. To do so blatantly disregards our innate ability for critical thought, a powerful tool for self-preservation. Bypassing our critical thinking process can tremendously alter our life course and have possibly catastrophic results. In the policing world, we relate this to target fixation. We are supposed to gather evidence to form an understanding of what happened, not what we believe happened. Fixating can often cause other potentially important details to be completely overlooked. One can only imagine the devastating consequences that could have on an investigation.

Thirdly, learn how to discuss uncomfortable topics and remain calm when doing so. Humans need to develop the ability to have rational conversations about issues that they find uncomfortable while remaining free of emotion. If we cannot converse without being angry or harboring resentment towards the person to whom we're speaking, how are we to progress as a civilization? There is no magic answer or inspirational quote for this. Progressing to find truth requires stepping outside your comfort zone and having difficult conversations. Start talking about things that make you uneasy. In the policing world, we often don't have a choice in this matter. We are in the business of addressing uncomfortable situations and navigating through them with tact and respect. We are taught in police training that our emotions are to be checked at the door when we're on duty and we are to strictly deal with the facts of a situation.

Finally, look for proof. Be on the lookout for those who speak with conviction but fail to provide evidence to support their claims. Surely, many police officers have found themselves in situations throughout their career where the story being told at the scene was not supported by the evidence present, yet the person telling the story was very convincing.

Evidence is a must when getting to the truth of any matter. Police officers are required to present evidence when making a claim and, ideologically speaking, only after this evidence is scrutinized can a conviction or acquittal be rendered. No judge would convict someone before hearing and assessing all evidence supporting the accusation.

With all this being said, our interactions should come from a place of compassion and curiosity. This is easier said than done, but making the effort to do so will only enhance our interactions with others. Two listening styles are commonly used: listening to understand, and listening to respond/refute. We should always strive to do the former. This is the only way to get to the bottom of what is fact and what is fiction. When we patiently listen to someone's point of view intending to understand them, we pave the way for a more open and informative conversation. We must also recognize that we are all human, and that we are all fallible and subject to reacting from emotion. This is where compassion comes into play.

There's no sugar-coating it: standing up for truth and speaking out requires concrete moral conviction. In a word, bravery. One must have a solid understanding of what they stand for and the reprisals they face for voicing their opinions.

If someone who wants to speak out is struggling to find their voice or experiencing trepidation, connecting with other strong-willed individuals with similar views is a good starting point.

As mentioned earlier, Police on Guard was a joining of like-minded people within the ranks of policing. Without each other, we are merely individuals, but together with our minds working as one, we are an army. When people who share similar values come together and act as one voice, the results are extremely powerful. This has proven to be true throughout this pandemic as groups from different countries, career paths, and walks of life that are fighting for truth and human rights continue to form and grow.

Police on Guard's message has always been focused on the importance of Canada's Charter of Rights and Freedoms, and how current orders instituted by our federal and provincial governments grossly violate it. The argument boils down to this: are these violations reasonable, or are they causing more harm?

Everyone has their own opinion on this, and only recently have the courts been brought into the equation. We are anxious and excited to have our claims and concerns heard in court. We are ready to see the other side of the narrative be formally addressed as various experts voice their educated opinions on behalf of Police on Guard for Thee, and all Canadians.

~ A written collaboration by members of Police On Guard For Thee

https://policeonguard.ca/

Chapter Thirteen

Throwing a Wrench in The Machine

By Shawn Jason

"My life is at risk. I know this. Of course it is. Anyone who pokes at the belly of the beast carries the risk of being eaten by the beast. I persist, though, because the threat to us all is far greater than my own personal risk." -- Shawn Jason

INTRO

My name is Shawn Jason. I am the creator of a crazy little project called Druthers. If you are not yet familiar, Druthers is a new independent newspaper that is not bought or controlled by giant corporate interests. It brings Canadians (and soon Americans too) the news, information, and perspectives that mainstream media ignores, belittles, or outright lies about.

It is deeply concerning to me, and to many others, how the majority of media outlets have entirely become propaganda machines for the establishment to push their health-destroying products and drive their humanity-destroying ideologies into the consciousness of society. Plus, with big tech giants admittedly censoring and outright deleting and banning voices that question the official story, we are heading into a dark place for humanity if we don't stop this sooner rather than later. And it's all under the guise of 'for your safety' and 'for the safety of others'.

We keep hearing 'trust the science.' But science doesn't work that way. We know this. A smart society is constantly analyzing and questioning data and science. It encourages discussion and debate. That's how science evolves and deeper discoveries are made. When all debate is shut down and only one thread of the story is 'allowed' to be heard by the population, that's not science. That's propaganda, and that is a dangerous thing for us all. Are you seeing this, too?

Have you read *1984* by George Orwell? His book seems rather prophetic when looking at the world in which we live right now.

And no, this is not some conspiracy theory. This is a conspiracy fact and it can be seen by anyone who gives a close, honest look. Just pick up a copy of Klaus Schwab's book *COVID-19: The Great Reset*. You know Klaus? The cartoon villain-looking guy who runs the World Economic Forum? Yeah, he tells us in black and white what he and his kind have in mind for all of humanity.

THEY CAN'T CENSOR PRINTED INFORMATION

A question that kept nagging at me and some friends was, "How do we get past the lies and censorship to give people important, alternative information and perspectives to look at?" That's when a friend planted a seed of thought in my mind.

He said, "Bro, we need to go old-school and print a newspaper."

The light bulb went on and five weeks after deciding to make a newspaper, we had crowd-funded, assembled, and printed 25,000 copies of the first issue (December 2020) of Druthers, and we started giving them out freely to people all over the Toronto area.

Incredibly, this paper was soooo well received! People stepped up to help give out papers. Some started writing articles. Others stepped up with donations. In a grass roots kind of way, this project and newspaper rapidly exploded all across the country. And now, eight months into this venture, we have printed and freely distributed nearly 1.7 million copies into every province and territory across Canada. This was entirely accomplished with generous donations and passionate volunteers.

Thousands of people now have stepped up to help Druthers happen. Turns out a lot of people are passionate about getting honest news and information to their fellow Canadians. Turns out there are a whole lot of people who see the bigger picture of what's happening to our country and they are so selflessly doing all they can to help change the path we are on before it is too late.

So, how do we change the path we are on? I think the answer is simple: Information. If people only receive the one-sided narrative, of course they are going to believe what they are being told. That's where Druthers comes in, to throw a wrench in the gears of the machine. Druthers provides alternative perspectives, and gives a platform to various experts and narratives of which the people should really be aware.

When enough people see and acknowledge there is a problem, we absolutely will come together and find solutions. We are many. We are strong. We are magnificent creators, and we can turn things around pretty quickly when enough people choose to. It is my hope that Druthers helps more people begin to question things more deeply.

AM I BRAVE?

Funny thing is that many people call me brave for speaking out against the establishment and printing this paper. And I suppose there is some validity to that. I am bringing attention to things that some very powerful and influential people won't like, and that's a threat to them and to their continued stranglehold on humanity, so of course that puts me at risk.

At the same time, though, if we don't take action and stop this agenda from rolling forward, we are going to see a terribly bleak, unpleasant future for all of humanity. Yes, for you, for me, for all of our families, and all of our loved ones; for literally everyone. Well, for everyone except the fraction of a percent at the top who will own and control practically everything on the planet.

As the World Economic Forum (remember Klaus) stated in a video they released and then later deleted: "You'll own nothing. And you'll be happy." They went on to say we will rent everything and it will be delivered by drone. This begs a very important question: if the people own nothing, who would own the things we rent? Our corporate overlords, of course. And they are creepily rubbing their hands together in anticipation while doing all they can to force this new reality upon us.

Social credit scores are coming (unless we stop it), just as they already have in some parts of China, which includes intense tracking and tracing of the people. It will be rolled out at first as a vaccine passport, which will never go away. Rather, the passport will evolve into the much stronger control mechanism it is designed to be, containing all of our info and our social scores based on how 'good' of a citizen we are, with 'bad' citizens not being able to access various services, events, travel, or other of life's pleasures.

There is a major push right now by the ruling class who wish to quite literally own and control everything on the planet. Everything! They are intentionally destroying the middle class. And with the middle class gone, who remains? There will be the few at the top owning and controlling everything, and everyone else who will be at the mercy and whim of those few at the top. Are we really going to stand by and let this happen? Is this really the world we want to leave for our children and grandchildren?

Personally, I wholeheartedly refuse to accept that reality being stuffed down our throats right now. I know we can create a far better future for all of humanity, but we are at a very monumental fork in the road. If we continue to blindly follow down the path on which we are being led, we will most certainly come to regret it, deeply. We MUST come together and stand together, NOW, and re-create our own new reality. I beg of you, every one of you reading this, please stand up with me and say NO MORE!!!

I don't consider it brave to do all I can do to stop this global takeover. Rather, I see it as short-sighted and naive to do nothing and to just hope things somehow go back to normal. I feel compelled into action for the sake of us all, despite the current risk to self, and I invite more people to join me in this way of thinking.

GOOD HEARTS HAVE BEEN HIJACKED

People are out there wearing masks and getting injected with an unproven, experimental substance, with most people doing it because they have been convinced it is what's best for their community. As admirable as that is, people's good hearts have been hijacked into doing things that are tremendously harmful for the community in the long run. Good, kind, caring people have been fooled into these actions. I pray more of those good hearts start to see the bigger picture and use their compassion to find the strength and resolve to stand up with the people, before it's too late.

Pretty much everyone by now must recognize there is something terribly wrong with the bigger picture. The majority are not speaking out or standing up yet, but more and more people are, and I pray this message helps more people step up already! We are watching life as we know it be destroyed right in front of our eyes and we must do anything and everything we can to make this stop, ASAP! As I see it, nothing matters more right now.

This is what gives me strength and courage despite the possible repercussions from the powers who ought not to be. Sure I may get 'taken out' due to this journey. I acknowledge that possibility and accept the risk. I just hope I've had enough effect in this world that it changes the current path we are on. And, if so, my passing would be perfectly fine. But please do not let my efforts and my life go to waste. Stand with me! When enough of us stand up, we WILL put an end to this and the risk to myself and to others will diminish. If we don't stand up in time, it is likely that my life will not be long and everyone else's life will become much less pleasant.

WE WILL WIN THIS

Fortunately, I very much believe we really are going to win this. We are watching more and more people all over the world who are banding together and standing together to make this insanity stop. Millions of people are taking to the streets in countries all around the world to call out against this attempt at a global takeover. I'd say it's time for North America to start standing together too, in a big way!

Enough with the manufactured divide, hate, anger, and judgment. We are not born hateful. We are born pure, free, loving, and kind. Almost all the hatred and anger in the world is massaged into us by the few at the top who know a humanity united is an incredible force and a serious threat to their positions of power. We must recognize this to overcome it. Most people are truly good inside and they wish good for others. When we reconnect with our earth family, we are an unstoppable creative force who can make anything happen. Corporate/government control is not the way to a happy, peaceful people. We must take the reins and consciously create the world we want to see.

As I see it, it is inevitable for humanity to win this. I am excited by what is happening, actually. The evils in this world are exposing themselves right now and more people are beginning to see. And only when we see can we make a conscious choice to fix it. I believe it is happening. I believe we are witnessing/experiencing an evolutionary leap in the consciousness of humanity right now, and that is highly exciting to me.

Yes, it is a sad time for many on an individual level, and all that suffering is painful to witness, but growing pains are to be expected and when we come through the other side of this, life will become so much more happy, peaceful, prosperous, and pleasant for all! That's my belief, vision, and direction of focus, anyway.

I am sure most of us can admit that life as we know it was already broken in many ways before 2020. There is no going back to normal. Too much has already changed. And I say, good! We don't want that normal back. The old normal saw far too much war, destruction, hunger, homelessness, mental illness, and physical ailments. We were guided into a strong "I" mentality and away from a "WE" mentality. This has caused much devastation in many ways among the world's population. All of it is driven by a soulless corporate culture which does not care for humanity. I want something far better for all. I presume you do too, right?

We must claim back our power. Own it. Stand in it. Use it. Both individually and collectively. We people are truly incredible beings (yes, you too). We are capable of so much more than any of us can even come close to realizing yet. But realizing that will only happen when we get along as one big earth family. And that will only happen when we rid ourselves of the evils who have been manipulating us for a very long time. Distract and divide. Divide and conquer. Conquer and control.

ARE WE READY?

Are we ready to open our eyes, acknowledge what is, and collectively stand up in the face of the beast and say no? Once we do, I am sure we will see it is much like the Wizard of Oz when they pulled back the curtain and discovered it was just a small man back there -- nothing scary at all.

Come on, humanity. Let's do this! The world really needs you.

Thank you. I love you.

Shawn Jason | Creator of www.druthers.net

Get involved. Help me with this cause. Nothing matters more right now! Visit www.druthers.net to learn more, or email info@druthers.net and one of our volunteers will connect with you.

About Shawn Jason:

Shawn Jason has been a long-time activist and a life-long rebel of sorts. Growing up in a small, rural town in Ontario, Canada, his curious and rebellious nature landed him in plenty of trouble as a teenager. He was never a 'bad' kid, he just didn't listen and do as he was told in the way most adults expected him to. He was happy doing his own thing and forging his own path through life, which led him through a myriad of unusual situations and experiences. He wandered a lot, living in dozens of places and working for over 60 companies before giving up on 'jobs' and embracing his entrepreneurial spirit. He has always been a lover of life and a believer in the power of unity in humanity. Late in 2020, he put aside all his projects to create this new, incredible, honest newspaper called Druthers.

Learn more about his project at www.druthers.net

Or follow him on Facebook at www.facebook.com/shawnjason

Chapter Fourteen

Red Pill Rapper

By Mitch Murphy

As I write this chapter, I find myself awestruck by the circumstance in which I type out the words. I'm currently leaving Kelowna, BC on a large Eagle Rider tour bus surrounded by dozens of Christian evangelicals, prophets, apostles, intercessors, and performers. As we drive through Highway 97 towards the Alberta border, we are accompanied by approximately ten other large pickup trucks, all of which bear flags flapping in the wind: Canadian flags, Gadsden flags, Battle for Canada flags, and a variety of slogans that include "F*ck Trudeau", "The Resistance", "Church is Essential" and other catchy things. It's a show of force, something that many in our community don't understand. I believe that as we drive through, there are many who are struck by fear at the sight of dozens upon dozens of unmasked locals (many of us unashamedly having white skin) gathered together in a public display that is a bold rejection of everything our government and top health officials have told us, and with a total disregard for everything we have been taught to believe throughout our entire education. For those who have a general trust for the system of which we are a part, they cannot seem to understand why we would do such things.

And on the surface, I suppose it is insane. You see, a number of weeks ago, the Jason Kenney Conservative Party of Alberta began putting disobedient pastors in jail. First James Coates, then Artur Pawlowski, and then Tim Stephens. This was when we started planning our trip to Alberta. We are bringing our outdoor worship protest into Alberta to show our government that we are not afraid and we will not be bullied into submission. We will worship, we will live free, and we're not sorry. However, before I tell you anymore, I suppose I should tell you a little bit about who I am, and how I got here.

I was born on March 5, 1996 in Summerland BC. I came into the world quiet, with a peaceful and curious gaze. My mother was concerned that I hadn't been crying like her two previous children. Upon further inspection, the doctor informed my mother that she had nothing to worry about. After a crisp smack on the bottom, I bellowed a tyrannical scream that echoed throughout the halls of the Penticton Hospital -- a pronounced yell that proved my formidable lung capacity. To my mother's delight, I had all my fingers and toes, and I had the German blonde hair and blue eyes that came from her ancestors as opposed to the dark eyes and black hair my father bore from his Irish parents.

I was the youngest of three siblings. My older brother was an awkward child with an eternally curious nature which kept him questioning everything as he grew up. My sister was a kind-hearted quiet girl with a wicked sense of humour. As we grew in the mountain ranges on the outskirts of Summerland, we made friends with the neighbourhood children and set up tire swings in the trees, threw pinecones at one another, and walked barefoot through the creek. It was an incredible childhood full of wonder and hardship, countless scraped knees and bee stings, and a childhood I wouldn't trade for all the money in the world.

I believe that I grew up with an intense love for freedom because I was given the opportunity to learn that if I climbed too far up a tree, the fall hurt that much more, and that if I went too fast on a dirtbike, the ruts in the path hit that much harder.

I was given the freedom to explore my boundaries and to expand my capabilities until the world shut it down and resulted in tears, scrapes, or bruises.

Many of the kids with whom I went to school were not awarded such a childhood. I was astonished when I went over to a new friend's house and would find them yelling horrible things at their mothers when asked to clean dishes, or crying when they weren't blessed with snacks. What I found most appalling was the rules. Rules. Rules. Rules. We weren't allowed to climb the trees, we weren't allowed to throw things in the yard, we weren't allowed to stay up late. We were always well-slept and our clothes remained clean, and I was always shocked by the abundance of electronics. At my house we had television and outdated gaming consoles, but at some of these houses they not only had the hottest new gaming consoles but specialty controllers, big screen TVs and surround sound, the first-person shooter games almost looked more real than reality, and it all made my head spin. I didn't mind following all the rules because the highly addictive video games made me feel like I was on fire! But I was always acutely aware that the lifestyle my family had was the correct one, and I was happy to come home to the mountain air and the liberty that came with it.

As I grew into manhood, I had an insatiable desire to learn about history, politics, and culture. I dove into the works of Adam Smith, Sam Harris, Joe Rogan, Owen Benjamin, and countless others. I had fallen away from my Christian roots, and I became a believer in New Age ideas that excused any and all of my vapid desires to sleep with women, drink myself into a blackout every night, and speak with a foul acuity that made anyone over the age of 40 curl their toes. I wanted a cause to stand for and I wanted to understand the world around me, but for many years my love for alcohol came before my education, career, and relationships.

I believe that the natural adrenaline I came to know in my childhood through healthy adventure had been replaced by drinking. This is why I moved to Edmonton to pursue a plumbing apprenticeship at the age of 18. I wanted to get my priorities in order and become a better man.

I worked hard for years, and on February 9, 2018 I had my last drink. I started going to AA meetings, and through the community setting I was able to acknowledge my problem and resolve it.

Over the years, my love for alcohol often calls me back to the bottle, but the meetings are always there, for which I am grateful. No more waking up wondering where I was, what I had done, and no more cleaning vomit off the bathroom floor before work! What an incredible life this is once sobriety is achieved. I had so much more time to use my clear thinking to listen to political podcasts and read philosophical literature. And it seemed the more I learned, the more it became obvious that something was wrong. This is when the rabbit holes really began.

As a young teenager, I was always interested in the crazy Alex Jones talking about a "pedophile island" and the thousands of engineers who claimed jet fuel couldn't melt steel beams, but I never took any of it too seriously. But here I was, a young man reading about Bill Gates buying up the majority of our farmland and claiming ownership of CN rail through stock exchanges, and I kept noticing trends . . .

Such as, why is it that every mainstream media outlet supports more war? Why is it that white people are always blaming their own race for current issues? Why does the "Conservative" party of Canada support the use of puberty blockers for children and toddlers?

These questions made me an unwelcome guest at certain dinner parties, but I didn't care, because while some were offended by my questions, they never claimed I was wrong for connecting the dots. They simply would say that I'm a racist, sexist, bigot, homophobe, etc.

After I had a strong grip on my sobriety, I convinced my girlfriend to move back to the Okanagan with me. I remember telling her things like "I think the supply chains are going to break down. We shouldn't live in a major city," and "We need to move somewhere where our neighbors smile and say hi!" I couldn't put my finger on it, but I knew something was wrong.

About three months after the move, we decided the relationship wasn't going to work, and she went back to Edmonton. About two months after that, we started hearing about this novel "coronavirus". I was dealing with some heartache and I was becoming increasingly frustrated watching the media encourage racially divisive movements like BLM and cheering on Trump while he escalated tensions with Iran while they smeared his supporters as racistsexistbigothomophobes.

So I went to Wentworth music in Kelowna, spent far too much money, and built a studio in the RV in which I was living. I made up my mind that I would become a rapper, because I knew something big was coming and I wanted to be a part of it. As the fear was ramping up in the media, I began staying up till 4 in the morning every night writing and practicing rap music. I didn't realize it at the time, but I believe God was convicting me of this mission so that I could make a difference when the time came.

Through that time, my sister and her husband were my support system. I showed them the insane music I was writing and they listened to me repeat the same lyrics with slightly different additives over and over and over again until they knew my songs better than I did. They sat with me as I cried, mourning not only the death of a relationship I thought I would be in for the rest of my life, but I was also mourning the country as the spirit of freedom in which I had thought we all believed died in front of me. I watched as almost every single church bent the knee to the fed and closed their doors during our nation's greatest time of need in my lifetime.

As “two weeks to flatten the curve” turned into “one month to slow the spread”, it became abundantly clear to me that this was going to be the biggest mobilization of the globalists in my lifetime. I didn’t know if Corona was deadly (in fact, I assumed it was going to be a deadly bioweapon) and I didn’t know what was going to happen but I knew it was time to fight. I sought out the closest protest I could find, which happened to be the CLEAR rallies run by the controversial David Lindsay. There I met a very large group of exceptional people. These folks all seemed to be aware of the depopulation agenda, child trafficking, and so many other important issues that are ignored by the mainstream. I had no idea that so many other people were aware! This was when I realized how important this movement would be, and that if we could all come together in unified opposition to the deep state, we would make big change in this country and in this world.

My first few months were incredibly challenging. I rallied with approximately 15-20 people who all appeared to be in their 60s, and we were widely despised by the public. Those driving by would spit at us, hurl terrible insults at us, and inform us that they hoped we would catch this virus and soon die. This was hard for me, but what was worse was that when I started posting pictures of our activism online, I immediately lost several childhood friends. Most of them wrote public essays on my Facebook informing me that I was a "super spreader" and that my views were going to kill everyone in my town. I was called every name in the book, and the common sentiment was the people's perception that we thought we were smarter than every doctor in the country.

However, no matter how many names these people called me, I refused to believe that closing small businesses and funnelling everyone into Costco was going to make us any safer. I refused to believe that by closing the churches (and AA meetings) we would be healthier as a nation. I refused to believe this would be a temporary loss of freedoms and that the impacts of the restrictions wouldn't be felt for generations to come. I also figured that if these people didn't want to be my friends over this, I would have lost them over something else anyway.

So, I kept writing offensive music and performing at rallies. I kept speaking out, and I kept making as much noise as possible. With time, I made new friends! I became close with Jordyn Montgomery, Chris Allnutt, Zaralea Mollard, Sarah and the Resistance, Joel Kelln, Ian Kotowich, Santana Yunker, Tamara Dinardo, James and Carla along with their children, and too many others to count.

Slowly but surely our rallies grew. Week after week, I would have someone else in my inbox offering quiet and distant support. Sometimes the support would be from old friends. Sometimes police or paramedics would reach out and they would say things like "I would love to join your rallies but I can't lose my job". I've never been more sure that I'm on the right side of history.

I also had some Antifa types email my corporate office telling them that I'm a "White supremacist Proud Boy COVID Denier" or something, which thankfully my boss laughed about. I guess nobody cares who you vote for when you need your toilet unclogged.

As time went by, we watched the rally grow and we watched the public have a change of heart. The spitting and jeering turned into honks of appreciation and thumbs up, our crowds got younger and more lighthearted, and our tactics got more refined. My friend Chris Allnutt (Host of the Allnutteral Raw Thoughts podcast) brought a big speaker system into the middle of the highway (right after the Kelowna bridge) and every Saturday afternoon we would rally right there in the middle of traffic. We had dance music going, and as the cars were stopped at the red light we would hand Druthers newspapers through their windows. I often performed through the speaker my anti-lockdown music, which was well received. I found more and more of a hunger for my unfiltered music. People were so used to NWO music that mine came as quite a shock, so when I put my album up for sale on my website, people actually bought it! Redpillnation.ca quickly turned into something that I thought I could grow. It seemed "The Redpill Rapper" brand was really going to work, so I kept at it.

So here I am, on tour bringing my message right into the belly of the beast. We will be meeting Derek Sloan and Maxime Bernier in Edmonton as we tour around Alberta and BC. And there is nowhere else I would rather be and nothing else I would rather be doing. Big thanks to Art Lucier for keeping "The Harvest" church wide open through constant harassment by the RCMP, Castanet, and Globalist News (just to name a few) and for believing in me when any other church would have tucked their tail between their legs and cowered at my message. Also a shout out to The Resistance, and to everyone who helped make it a success.

You can listen to my podcast "The Redpill Rapper Show" and buy my music at Redpillnation.ca

Stay Strong Canada.

Mitch Murphy // The Redpill Rapper

About Mitch Murphy - Red Pill Rapper

Unrestrained by any corporate overlords, Mitch Murphy is a free thought powerhouse who stretches the limit of what society is ready to hear. A free speech warrior who knows no boundaries, his fearless nature is exemplified as his Gadsden cape billows with every motion, and the sharp edge behind his words leaves no doubt about where he stands. Mitch Murphy is truly a man of the people, a patriot, and a Christian who leads with conviction above all else.

You can listen to his podcast, "The Redpill Rapper Show", on Bitchute, Youtube, and various streaming services (dodging the thought police as much as possible), and his music is for sale at Redpillnation.ca, along with merchandise that promotes the message of freedom, liberty, and righteousness.

As we slip further into authoritarianism, it becomes clearer every day that people like Mitch really will have to be thrown into the Gulag before they quiet down.

And it would appear he's only going to get louder until that day comes.

Redpillnation.ca

Chapter Fifteen

Every Word Matters

By David Pilz

'Be impeccable with your word'. D Ruiz

World-renowned teacher and author Don Ruiz wrote and published the book *The Four Agreements*, wherein he suggested that if we merely follow a very simple formula our lives would benefit significantly. At the top of the list is the first agreement in the protocols: Be Impeccable With Your Words

What does this actually mean? If you explore the teachings, he goes on to offer up some guidelines like 'Say only what you mean' and to 'Avoid using words to speak against yourself or to gossip against others', ideally to only 'use your words for truth and love'.

Is it really enough to merely be honest and kind to ourselves and others with our words? Can our whole world really transform merely because we are speaking our authentic truth in an altruistic loving manner? Can a person heal themselves physically with mere words? Can a person actually heal themselves and others merely with their honest words? Psychology and sociology strongly suggest that spoken words can indeed have a powerful impact on our self-image and lifetime confidence. Can a supportive parent empower their child's growth authentically with words?

Neuro-linguistic programming (NLP) is one among many courses that a person can take that will teach them that words do indeed have power. Specific words create a predictable response from all those that hear them and placing those powerful words into a specific order within a spoken or written sentence will have an even greater impact. A person can create sentences, songs, poetry, and speeches meant to elicit very specific responses from their audience by choosing very specific words and placing them in specific order within a sentence structure. Heck, every mom in the world learns very quickly to offer their children a list of choices that she has pre-chosen rather than allowing the children to suggest options. I.E., 'tonight you can have a bath either before your homework, or afterwards' implies that the child has the independence to choose for themselves. Meanwhile, Mom has already narrowed down the only options the child believes are available and begins managing the execution of those options. The right words used in the right order at the right time compel adults to behave in a similar manner to instructions they might normally reject. In this example, a loving mom is authentically hoping to achieve her blatant agenda of teaching her children about hygiene, personal responsibility, and individual choices. Both parent and child participate in the exchange because Mom is ultimately in charge, the posture goes to Mom, and we can assume most moms would use these techniques benevolently, but what happens when the posture isn't benevolence? These very tools that are familiar to us can indeed be used to manipulate, incite, and exploit those that assume benevolence where it doesn't exist.

The speed of sound is 343 meters per second as it ripples outward in ever-widening circles away from the sound's creation and never stops. Large portions of every noise, sound, or conversation you have ever had are still broadcasting outward into the universe. Sounds themselves have a metaphysical and physical influence on every aspect of the human experience. Music can encourage healing and wholesomeness, passion and creativity, destruction and inspiration, with or without any accompanying spoken word. When we start interjecting very specific words with precision and skill, we can capitalize and expand upon those musically inspired human responses. The different genres reflect symbiotically many of the human experiences and cultures that motivate them, while the songwriters look perpetually for the perfect song and the perfect blending of word and sound to inspire a singular response from the listening audience.

174 Hertz – removes pain

285 Hertz – Influences energy field

396 hertz - Liberates you of fear and guilt

417 Hertz - Facilitates change

432 Hertz - Miracle tone of nature

528 Hertz - Repairs DNA

639 Hertz - Heals Relationships

741 Hertz - Awaken intuition

862 Hertz - Attracts soul tribe

963 Hertz - Connect with light and spirit

Organizations like Centerpointe University, Rhine University, and military Coordinate Remote Viewing programs have been exploring the influence of frequency and vibration on human physiology and psyche. They weren't merely looking for a physically devastating weapon that a focused sound manipulation can provide. They were also looking at how sound and frequency influences the mental and psychological aspects of soldiers and patients. The science on which they have spent many years and many millions of dollars to acquire proves there is no doubt that exposing a subject to specific frequencies can have an impact on them. Sounds can heal and support, and they can potentially even incite supernatural abilities to otherwise normal humans. Sounds can also distract, confuse, and destroy a normal functioning human.

Through these explorations, we've learned much about our world and how sound and frequency play a significant daily part in our human experience. In the 1930s, music was changed purposefully from being predominantly produced at 432Hz to 440Hz. Notably, 432Hz is a frequency that has universally symbiotic principles shared with the Fibonacci, Schumann Resonance, chakras, pi, and more. If you have an opportunity to listen to music played in 432hz compared to 440Hz, I'm sure you will notice the hair-raising differences in the fullness and metaphysical properties of the sound. Some theories surmise there may have been some awareness of this knowledge when the 440Hz was decided upon for all global music production. If this is true, then this would be a clear example of how something as inspiring, healing, and supportive for human growth as music has been diffused into something potentially manipulative. In my opinion, music is equally as powerful a miracle to our dimension and species as is spoken language.

Every parent knows that Mom can sometimes ask, verbally push, and even yell at their kids without any response or even acknowledgement, which is often how Mom develops her NLP skills mentioned previously. She learns to use her words effectively, almost strategically, but when Dad says the exact same words, the child responds differently. It's not just the spoken words, of course, it's the tone, the vibration. They might even have a closer relationship with their mother but the deeper 'dad voice' has an autonomic response in young children that carries through adulthood. The masculine tone instinctively implies a paternal authority, an instinctive impulse that can later be exploited by others who want to imply paternal authority in your life. When someone speaks with authority, specifically speaking in those low masculine 'Walter Cronkite' tones, we tend to listen, believe, and even obey instinctively.

Jon Kelly, a reverse speech expert with whom I've worked a couple of times over the years, has a technique where he records someone speaking and then by playing the recording backwards he is able to discern specific hidden truths that the speaker reveals in their 'backwords'. It might sound a little like we are playing an old LP recording backwards to receive hidden messages from the devil, as the technique is similar. In playing the speaker's words backwards, all of us were able to clearly discern how the person really felt about a discussed topic in spite of the flowery 'forewords' shared eagerly with us. There was even some specific information the speaker had shared buried backwards in the spoken word. The speaker admitted that he had been thinking about the specific information that the reverse speech technique exposed but didn't want to gossip or slander so he chose to withhold. He was disturbingly surprised to witness along with all of us that he had actually shared the info in reverse. I wonder how many political speeches should be played backwards and what those recordings might reveal under this scrutiny. Jon himself has received ample criticisms and dismissals along his pseudoscience explorations, but there are many first-hand witnesses to the fascinating work he has done and will continue to do.

In my opinion, words and language are the highest measurable forms of intellect. All manner of living beings have ways to communicate with the world around them. From primal mating calls to the ancient songs of whales as they communicate literally across the planet with one another, every living thing communicates a language. The most commonly spoken language amongst humans on the planet today is English, or at least a dialect of English that has evolved from centuries of global commerce to become a common trading tongue. This current version of spoken English is a bit of a mongrel language though, having no specific ancestry because it is certainly not the Queen's nor exclusively western English. English is then followed closely by Mandarin on the most commonly spoken languages chart, along with Hindi and Spanish. What makes these other languages different is they are ancient languages that have evolved into their current incarnations with the strong ongoing connection to a community, a culture, and/or a creed. Spanish is itself a language that reflects the conglomeration of numerous cultures coming together over many decades of conquest, war, and integration, but it still has many of the old tones buried in the speech. The ancient tones spoken that make up these ancestral languages have been around for a very long time and literally vibrate differently when spoken.

For example, the ancient Sumerians had over 400 characters that made up their alphabet, and each character had a history or a legend, so each individual letter brought rich history and sophistication. In direct comparison, the mere 26 characters involved in the English language has us comparably grunting at one another because regardless of how big those words accumulate we are ultimately limiting our communication spectrum by limiting our baseline.

The elimination of language is one of the most effective ways to induce a culture towards ultimate extinction, as it has been said that language is the accumulated power of those people who speak it. There are many folks who feel this is not just a romantic notion but an opportunity (for ill or for good will) to access a vulnerable space of a culture. I've received extensive teachings as a lodgekeeper over the years, and in those teachings is a common understanding of the power behind any spoken words shared in sacred places, along with the songs and their impact on the intent/outcome of the ceremony. Maybe those old languages are understood better by the ancestral spirits that also spoke them? Maybe those old tones had influence on the world in a way that new ones don't? Maybe the most significant influence that those old ancestral tones have on a person can be found in our genetics, in our DNA.

Is it enough to merely speak or sing in an old language to gain access to the strengths of those tones, or is it important to have an ancestral connection to the specific language that you are speaking? In my personal experiences, I can say that I receive a deeper understanding of songs and teachings when taught along with all the subtle nuances of the culture from which it is spoken. Context is important for mental understanding, but I feel strongly that sharing appropriate language and tones inspires communion. Many of the indigenous teachings are shared through song exclusively, because it is understood that memory is empowered when we sing the words versus speaking them. The 'Hooked on Phonics' education system is also based on this premise. I suspect that by including song to our words we invite both the left and right hemisphere of our brains to participate. Nature responds instinctively to those old tones. I am a being of nature.

As a human, each one of our organs vibrates at a specific frequency, and each individual human will also emanate a slightly unique frequency from each organ. Adding all those frequencies together is like creating an orchestra one instrument at a time. That compilation of frequencies can be identified as our 'song', as unique to each person as their fingerprints. People can sense this song in others, some folks being more adept at sensing it than others, but we all subconsciously connect with one another in this way. A vibe? A feeling? An intuition about a person?

A well-trained metaphysical healer can sometimes intuit where the body needs tuning to empowered harmony in the same manner a conductor might tune an orchestra, by applying trained senses to interpret the ongoing vibrations being received.

After exploring all these different expressions of communication in our world, there is an understanding that communication takes place on many levels of awareness at once. Body language, subconscious interpretations of vibrations in our auric emanations, song, nuance, inflection, cultural and social constructions, and much more contribute to every conversation. Even those methods of communication that don't use spoken or written words access a part of our personal experience because communication always has an intent, an agenda. Morse code is tapped out in a string of a seemingly nonsensical manner to anyone except another who can interpret those dot, dot, dashes into relevant information. Sign language for the deaf doesn't even rely upon sound to communicate as clearly as any other form of communication. Hieroglyphics, glyphs, and cave paintings have been around for as long as we can perceive, and they continue well into our technological age as a new generation of humans relies heavily upon emoji shapes to communicate fully-developed conversations. Flags and heraldry continue to inform significant amounts of information at a glance while universal traffic signs, shapes, and colours keep people moving along regardless of the country they are in.

We communicate in so many forms between one another, why do we even need words at all? In my opinion, words are ideally meant to communicate what we are feeling, thinking, and experiencing with others in a somewhat permanent manner, so this communication method can be passed from person to person without misinterpretation. As each person shares their experiences and opinions with others, they are hopefully being honest and as open as they can be because ultimately all perspectives are unique. We each have individual experiences and personal journeys that influence those perspectives that others may not have had, and one of the ultimate purposes of communication is to share those experiences so others can gain the benefit of our experiences.

When two people share their experiences, expertise, knowledge, and wisdom with words, they are ultimately hoping to expand their understanding of the topic being discussed. We all experience life and events differently, even if we witness the exact same event according to the 'theory of relativity'. Every part of your personal journey encourages you to experience the world through your own lens. Thus, you will have a bias slanted towards your own personal perspectives. We share with others so we can gain their bias and their knowledge, and they do the same looking for our bias. Even when both parties speak honestly and accurately about their experience, it's so very common for there to be slight or even dramatic differences in their shares. THE truth is so often found by comparing both stories and agreeing on something in the middle upon which everyone can agree. Because the ultimate truth is always somewhere in the middle.

Ultimately, words (communication) are purposefully used to share our truths so that we can compare those truths to another person's version and expand our own accurate awareness of our world. This can only happen if both parties are resolutely speaking from a place of 'their truth', but also attaching an 'esoteric question mark' to the end of their statements -- a subtle, or not so subtle, asking of another person's truth to validate or add additional information to our own current understandings.

So, what happens when communication becomes a weapon to exclusively promote an agenda? Any good salesman can tell you that having training in appropriate word and even body language use can make a big difference in their bottom line. What happens when there is censorship of even one person's perspectives? Propaganda has infiltrated every sector of communication and media on the planet. It's been there for a while, getting better and better with each new generation of human consumer guinea pigs providing endless information to those who compile it, looking for even better ways to motivate your choices with their words. The very approach to communication is about control, not connection. When this happens, the discovery of 'The TRUTH' is not only difficult but potentially impossible. Those that understand 'gaslighting' as a tool to promote their own ideals and agendas exclusively are obviously not utilizing communication for truth but are exploiting the primal (sacred) essence of communication for malice. How do we protect ourselves from manipulation? From lies and deceit?

The science of kinesiology is the exploration of the body's connection to the world. It is understood that the body is hardwired to the universe in such a manner that it always knows the truth about any topic, event, or situation. Used predominantly in the western world for diagnosing allergies, kinesiology is a tool that can be used for dowsing, metaphysical awareness, and physiological communications with a person's 'truth'. We can often get muddled in our mind and sometimes triggered emotionally about opposing narratives presented to us, but our body knows 'truth'. The premise of measuring truth with this technique is that the universe refuses to support anything anti-life, and the body clearly defines lies, untruths, and miscommunication as anti-life. The practitioner or client will attempt to resist against an opposing force while focusing on a specific topic. For example, hold an arm in the air, then have someone push down on your arm while making statements about specific things, IE "I am allergic to cats." If you are indeed allergic to cats, the arm you are holding aloft will resist the opposing push downward, but if you are not allergic to cats the arm will weaken against the opposing resistance. The body always knows and will only support truth with energy, chi, and strength.

After years of teaching these techniques, using them personally and professionally, I can attest that the greatest interference in achieving 100% accuracy from kinesiological readings is the subject's inability to remain open to the answers provided. We can so clearly convince ourselves that our perspective on something is so absolutely 'the truth' that we create resistance and blocks to receiving information outside of that perspective. Cognitive dissonance is the most recent term used to describe this response, but humans have been fooling themselves for a very long time and outright rejecting external information that contradicts their own inner narrative, regardless of any physical or empirical evidence.

Kinesiology can be a tool to help a person understand when something isn't quite right, or to know when someone is lying to them, but it won't automatically provide the correct answers. For me personally, after years of developing my own inner kinesiology, I can accurately tell when someone is lying to me but I might not be able to identify what they are specifically lying about or what the 'truth' of their deceit actually is. Even if the speaker believes what they are saying is true, kinesiology will respond to a lie as a lie. Partial truths are so often the tool of a betraying manipulator. They speak just enough truth for it to be received as such while also omitting context or twisting important contributing factors to meet their agenda.

To be impeccable with our word, as inspired by the teacher Don Ruiz, is, in my opinion, so much more than speaking words honestly. A person's word is a sacred sound that they emit outward into the universe from within their inner core, and if those spoken words are 'truthful', then that truth will be felt and empowered by the inner kinesiology of all those that hear them. We can tell when a musician is authentically sharing versus merely making noise, even if they are singing our favorite song. So, too, can we know when something we hear doesn't quite ring true.

The journey towards becoming impeccable begins with 'I' statements. Instead of expressing any form of generalization like 'when those men jump to conclusions', a person instead states 'when I jump to conclusions.' This instantly creates a personal connection to the ongoing dialogue and encourages us to share our own personal experiences instead of regurgitating what we've heard from others. 'I' statements instantly remove the capacity to gossip in its many forms and implicitly encourages us to share only our personal 'truth'. When conversations get real and personalized, clear communication is inevitable. If everyone is sharing their personal truth transparently, 'the truth' can most often be found somewhere near the middle.

Being impeccable with my word is what others hear from me even when I'm not speaking. People can feel connection instinctively from me when I anchor into my words, courageously sharing my ultimate truths in my personal pursuit of authenticity and accuracy. I'm convinced others will feel this from you also.

The entire reason, the very purpose for the miracle of communication to exist, is to discover 'the truth' that exists somewhere outside of our individually limited spectrum. Whenever I start using terms like 'they' or 'them', or generalize others, then I dilute my ability to empathize or be in connection with the source of the information I am sharing. A separation immediately exists that prevents 'us' from happening. A person who has integrity will 'vibrate' differently to those around them than someone who does not have it, and anyone walking impeccably will feel that inconsistency and disharmony dramatically. Yes, I'm talking about intuition and metaphysical awareness, but I'm also speaking about that black and white 'gut feeling' or 'gut intelligence' with which everyone is born. Even beyond the protective mechanisms of psychic evolution we can all instinctively feel incongruity in the world. If something doesn't feel quite right, it probably isn't. My advice is to ask questions until it does.

About David Pilz:

David Pilz is a Canadian-born author, speaker, certified master healer, alchemist, shaman, metaphysical doctor, consultant, and instructor who has spent well over 30 years in the metaphysical development field. His published works include *The Metaphysical Manual Series; Social Work for the Afterlife* documentaries; endless newspaper articles; interviews; and blog posts. His greatest joy is empowering others to achieve their fullest metaphysical potentials and he has literally years of experiential training behind him to help eager students achieve success. David has fostered a unique relationship within Indigenous communities as a respected bundle carrier and elder mainly because his own personal communions so closely resemble their teachings, but his ultimate goal is to personally achieve alchemic balance. David continues to offer consultations, treatments, metaphysical tools, and teachings through his thriving practice currently based out of Vancouver, Canada. DavidPilz.com

Ommanna.com

Chapter Sixteen

Truth, Freedom, and Health

By Nordia German

Born in Montreal, Quebec and raised by Jamaican parents, I was brought up with good moral values. Respect your elders, thou shalt not lie and steal, "Do unto others as you would have them do unto you", stand up to those who challenged you, never be the one to start a fight and never lay your hands on someone until they do, etc. I knew some of those valuable lessons would be of great use one day, especially in standing up to tyrants.

I always wondered where I got my semi-fierce, brave attitude from. I guess the stereotypical thinker would say, "Well, you are Jamaican, of course!"

Okay, all jokes aside, who is Nordia German? She is a passionate health junkie who passes most of her spare time reading and researching health topics. She's always trying to find the latest cutting-edge research on longevity, disease reversal, and all that fun stuff.

I've been working as a registered nurse for over four years. The reason I came into this profession is, like for most nurses, the need to care for and help those who are unable to help themselves. If you had asked me ten years ago to apply to nursing school, I would have given you the strangest look. I still wonder today what exactly triggered me to enroll in nursing school. Was it my mother's marvellous stories on how she cared for the sick and vulnerable and how she spoke of the love, compassion, and connection she had for them? Was it my grand-aunt passing due to a medical error? At this point, all I know is that I am forever grateful to God to have put me on this path.

I know exactly where I got my brave heart; my parents. A few years ago, I realized at what point I am my mother's daughter. In the same way she advocated for her residents/clients I also advocate for mine: calling out the negligence and all forms of malfeasance and will do all in her power to defend them. The stories are endless. Love you, Mom.

And my wonderful Pops, my dad, I can now say that I get my calm side from him, being able to stay cool, calm, and collected during adversity. I couldn't say that a few years ago. It's all personal development, on which I am continuously working. Always finding ways to upgrade my life and to become a better version of myself.

Before this *casedemic*, I was working in a hospital and in homecare through an agency. I remember being really busy because at the same time I was pursuing my holistic health studies. Not much has changed, might I say. I was a self-taught integrative health practitioner and spent most of my free time studying and researching work from top integrative and functional medicine doctors such as Dr. Bland, Dr. Mercola, and Dr. Mark Hyman, to name a few. The main reason I got into alternative health studies is because I wanted to educate my family, friends, and community so they could become their own doctors and advocate for their health. I wanted to show them what was possible and how it can be simple to reverse diseases if they would just remove toxicities and impurities and replace them with the right nutrients. I never learned that in nursing school, which follows a pharmaceuticals model, not natural alternatives and not telling clients and patients how to get to the root cause of their ailments. I can attest to that because I was able to reverse my chronic conditions naturally by getting to the foundation of what was causing my symptoms. Adios cortisone and acid blockers! :)

Now I am focusing on my studies, my projects, coaching my community, and working part-time as an RN. I must not forget that I am investing a lot of time, brainstorming, and thinking of new ways to contribute to Canadian Frontline Nurses. As I am writing this chapter, Jessica Di Giovanni (my soul nurse sister from Quebec), other organizers, and I are planning a rally in front of the College of Nurses of Quebec. We are planning on gathering many healthcare professionals, teachers, and police officers. This way we can bring much awareness to the general public and have our stories and voices be heard.

The Casedemic

It was Friday, March 13, 2020. I remember going through my emails in the employee break room, checking if an upcoming health fair I was looking forward to attending was cancelled. My assumptions were right: it was cancelled, along with other public events. I also remember many of my work colleagues panicking, not knowing if their daycares would be closed, wondering and preparing for the worst. That would mean it would leave them no other option but to stay home until they figured out who would look after their little ones. Well, here comes more understaffing and extra work overload. On March 14, Quebec's Premier Legault officially declared a public health emergency, which was supposed to only last ten days.

I must admit, the government got me for about a good week. I was the only one wearing an N95 mask in the grocery store. It was something else, I tell you. I got those strange looks. I was telling myself, "Well, if there is a deadly virus out there, I have to protect myself." I swear, as I am writing this I am laughing out loud. The madness! Well, Francois Legault, you got me, but not for long.

What made me realize this was a whole *scamdemic*? The fact that I loved to read books and articles, and to research a variety of health topics, helped me see the scam behind this so-called "pandemic". One of the first questions I asked myself was, 'Why is our government asking the population to wear any type of face covering to "protect themselves and others"?' It made absolutely no sense. All masks are not created equally. The College of Nurses of Quebec questioned me on this topic and asked me if I was against mask-wearing. More on Quebec College of Nurses (OIIQ) interrogation in a bit.

I felt it was my duty, not only as a nurse who is here to protect the general public but also as a concerned human being, to share my findings on what they are calling COVID-19 and everything surrounding health as it is my passion and devotion. If there are oppositions to the common narrative, there needs to be public debate. We had none of that! So, I decided to use Facebook and Instagram to share what I was learning and discovering because the public must stay informed, and we definitely cannot rely on our government nor the media to educate us on health because of their biases and their one-size-fits-all approach.

Many of my friends on FB knew I was an RN. However, I never publicize my status and I tend not to give my opinion, just facts. I was surprised that I had no opposition. No one wanted to debate nor did anyone even question what I was posting. I did, however, get messages supporting what I was saying. In addition, I am grateful to say, up until this day I did not experience any family or friendship conflicts when I educated them on topics surrounding COVID. I also brought up mask-wearing and testing with work colleagues and they were always willing to hear what I had to say, but nothing more. They still went along with the "protocols", even though it made no sense.

In June 2020, I decided to close my Facebook and focus more on myself. It was hard to keep up with new information. I felt I was being bombarded. Moreover, I saw what was coming: the vaccine mandates and other immoral measures that would probably force me to quit conventional nursing. I took it into my own hands and decided to venture out for other streams of income. I had to find a way out! So, from June until October, I learned network marketing and financial investment, I improved my financial literacy, and I figured out how I can generate other income so I could quit my job and dedicate my time and energy to my health studies to better help and serve my community.

Then, on August 19, 2020, at exactly 2:55 PM, while I was at work, I received a missed call from the OIIQ advising me of a complaint an individual had filed about a few posts on my Facebook feed. I was not surprised, knowing the history behind regulatory bodies and other health practitioners who had their licenses revoked by their colleges for questioning and defending patients' rights. I was then sent an email with a date and time for my virtual interrogation, which I later postponed. I made sure to gather all the information I needed, consulted with a well-known lawyer, and spoke with one of my mentors and a holistic psychologist for guidance. I remember wanting to quit and hand in the towel. I was so disgusted by the profession, I honestly no longer wanted to work as a conventional nurse. I no longer wanted to be under a regulatory body that does not respect its code of ethics.

At that time, there were no other nurses with me on the frontlines battling this fight. I had to be smart about my decisions and what to answer during the interrogation.

On Tuesday, September 15, at 10:00 AM, I was surprised at the questions that were asked. “As a nurse, you are not to educate the public on immunity” was a shocking comment the assistant from the OIIQ made. She was telling me that it is the leader of this province and his team of so-called specialists who educate the public on the immune system. As nurses, we are to educate the public with the right information and provide evidence that supports what we are saying. I did provide evidence!!! I even sent them scientific literature. But the college never got back to me on what I had sent to them. Strange, right?

During the questioning, I felt alone and felt like I had no choice but to tell them what they wanted to hear. So, I agreed, but under duress! I felt as though not only my freedom of expression but, even worse, my freedom of conscience was taken away from me. One of the worst feelings ever! This was my first run-in with the college. Before this, I was in good standing.

Thursday, October 22 was the day I received a letter of my file closure and that I could pass in front of the disciplinary committee and potentially face disciplinary actions if I was to recommit the same action. Well, today, I say BRING IT ON! I am ready to fight this one and I now have an army standing by my side because, after all, I am doing what is right!

Being a part of Canadian Frontline Nurses since December 2020 has been a blessing. The group has given me so much love and support. I am blessed and ever so grateful to have met Sarah and Kristen. They motivated me to speak my truth.

I decided to publicly speak out on May 1, 2021 at a rally in Montreal. I couldn't have done it without the support of my soul sister, Jess. I was hesitant, but she gave me the courage and drive. OMG, was I happy after speaking up! It was a rush. I highly encourage everyone to speak out and not hold themselves back. The feeling is so gratifying. Trust me, just do it! We were interviewed by David Menzies from Rebel News. I then decided to open back up my previous Facebook account and started where I left off, speaking the truth and informing my community.

It's important to spread information in every way that we can. Social media is a good tool to get your message out there. However, there has been an increase in censorship. With that being said, we (Canadian Frontline Nurses) decided to go on a cross-Canada tour to spread awareness, to inspire and educate the people, making it harder for the technocrats to censor us. What an amazing, unforgettable experience that was.

To end, I would like to say how grateful I am to be able to write a chapter and tell my story. I am encouraging everyone to empower themselves, to be their own advocate, and to take responsibility for their own health, empowering informed self-care and standing up for what is right. And, to my fellow health practitioners, we must respect and encourage freedom of choice and informed consent, and we must pride ourselves to be ethical advocates.

And remember truth, freedom, and health. They are all interconnected. You cannot have one without the other.

About Nordia German:

Nordia German, a registered nurse and Integrative Health Coach from Montreal, Quebec, has been practicing nursing for four years. She is on the Board of Integrative Medicine, is a member of Vaccine Choice Canada, and is a member of the Canada Health Alliance. She has a huge passion for holistic health and functional medicine and is continuously learning, every day.

Nordia was silenced by her college in September 2020 for posting on her private social media page, informing the public on a variety of health topics such as mask-wearing, vaccine ingredients, and alternative medicine. She is honoured to be fighting alongside other members of Canadian Frontline Nurses and others who stand by sound ethical practices, and to be part of a new health revolution. She is determined to help bring back real health because, as she states, "We live in a sick care system."

She is on a mission to empower many people to take ownership of their health as she did. Nordia once suffered from a few chronic conditions, gave her body the right nutrients, and is no longer a prisoner of these so-called "dis-eases". Informed self-care is what she promotes, as she knows we all have the power to heal. 💚

Nordia is always open to help out her community and is always in a place of service. She can be reached via email at nordiagerman@hotmail.com

Chapter Seventeen

Standing in Truth at 17

By Callie Ocean

Hi. My name is Callie, and I am a proudly unvaccinated 17-year-old. I moved from Squamish to West Vancouver in 2019. I have attended West Vancouver Secondary School (WVSS) for the past two years and graduated this year, 2021 - a year early. I explain to the reader why in this chapter. I also think it is important for the reader to know that I do not have any social media.

How I Knew COVID Was a Lie

I am so lucky that my parents, especially my mom, have taught me to question and decipher all information I hear, whether it's from a doctor, a teacher, or the news. This year I have met a lot of people of all ages and I can say that neither they nor I know anyone who has died of COVID. If this was a real pandemic, people would be dying left, right, and center all over the streets; ambulance sirens would constantly be on; and hospitals would actually be full, but they are not. This is clearly a fake pandemic that is being exaggerated and made to look real and believable by the news, social media, the medical system, the government, and the school system. That is why many people sadly can't see through this illusion and are believing this big lie. All these organizations and institutions share the exact same mainstream opinions about COVID. I really wonder why. Opinions and information published by doctors, vaccinologists, and pathologists that counter the mainstream narrative are being censored and suppressed. As well, these professionals are being discredited or labeled as crazy conspiracy theorists, anti-maskers, and anti-vaxxers. It's suspicious and shows that the real truth is being hidden from the people. I know that this whole COVID thing has absolutely nothing to do with the health and well-being of the people. It's hurting the people. It has everything to do with control, money, and power. I know that this truth is too big to hide and it will come out.

Social Life

Prior to COVID, I was lucky to have made friends with three other teens at school. I was so excited and I thought I had finally found my friend group. We texted and hung out at the mall and went for coffee. Then when COVID hit and masks started to become popular, all of my friends wore masks except for me. They asked why I didn't wear a mask and I said that for medical reasons I have an exemption.

They seemed fine with it at first, though as the year went on my friends were becoming increasingly more afraid of COVID. They were beginning to judge me and to peer-pressure me to wear a mask whenever we went out. I was also constantly being pressured by store employees to wear a mask. It was hard, but I did my best to stand up for myself and say no to all the mask pressure in a kind manner. COVID made me realize how different I was from my friends and how little we had in common. They loved talking about COVID rules, school work, social justice politics, and just meaningless superficial small talk.

I couldn't share my real opinion because they would judge and think badly of me. It drove me crazy. Then in December 2020, all of my friends were masking alone outside. That's when I knew it was time for me to let go of the group. I didn't have another friend until the middle of spring. I met a girl in my yoga PE class. We talked for a while and found we had a lot in common. Even though we have different opinions about COVID, we are still friends. As well, this summer I have started to meet some like-minded young people through our local freedom rallies and it has been great!

My Last Year of High School

In the beginning of my Grade 11 year, everyone was wearing masks. For the first month, I wore a mask because I really wanted to fit in and be liked by everyone. I noticed that my mental and physical health were suffering and I knew I could not continue to wear one. With my mom's help, we went to the principal and I got an exemption. He supported the exemption but said that I have to walk outside between classes. At first, going maskless was really hard and it was scary to stand up for myself.

Surprisingly, I was never bullied by students. Maybe that's because I am not on social media. But many of the teachers bullied me. Some teachers respected my exemption and some bullied me on a daily basis. Sometimes I was bullied by the same teacher multiple times in a day. It was just so bad, to the point where I walked in the halls with headphones on listening to music because I didn't want to engage and get yelled at.

There is one particular story out of many that I would like to share:

For the first day of my Grade 11 English class, the teacher took us to the library to listen to the librarian present about book topics. As I entered the library, I noticed everything had been spaced out for distancing. I sat in the front of the classroom.

The librarian began by talking about the importance of wearing masks and using sanitizers.

She then looked directly at me and said, "Which means you should be wearing your mask. I will give you a few seconds to put it on."

I weakly replied, "I am exempt for medical reasons."

She said, "There are no exemptions. Go to the back of the classroom."

I sat there frozen to the spot. I couldn't move.

Then she said more aggressively than the first time, "I will not continue speaking until you go to the back of the class."

I walked to the back of the class and sat down. I made eye contact with some kids in my class. They gave me the typical blank look. I sat there on the verge of tears, feeling so angry, upset, and humiliated. In that moment, I felt so put on the spot and I wish I would have stood up for myself.

The library incident in November was the turning point for me. I was so done with school, with the brainwashing and the COVID stuff. School was just bringing me down whenever I was there. I felt so anxious, to the point where I had panic attacks all the time and felt angry, depressed, and extremely stressed. I had to get out of what felt like a prison. I had to graduate. I decided I was going to do Grade 11 and 12 in the same year, as I had some extra credits from extracurricular activities from my Grade 10 year. I told my parents and my school counselor my plan. At first, they didn't agree, though when they saw nothing could change my mind, they eventually supported me.

Luckily, the second half of the school year got better. The great news is that with time, standing up for myself and speaking my truth got easier. I could stand my ground and say quietly but assertively, "I have a medical exemption. If you have a problem, please talk to the principal." Teachers began to realize that no matter how much they bullied and pushed me around I would not comply with their rules.

It brought me hope when I noticed a few kids at school this year took off their masks, though they were quickly shut down by teachers and continued to comply. The teacher discrimination and bullying at school was so bad, and the ironic thing is that they are breaking the anti-bullying rules they themselves created. I really feel that everyone needs to be aware of the discrimination and that action needs to be taken.

School System Brainwashing and Indoctrination

I attended a Waldorf School until Grade 4, where they encourage free speech and independent and critical thinking. However, I noticed a change when I went to public school. I am very intuitive and always had a gut feeling that there was some agenda behind what we were learning. I have always felt that something was seriously not right with the public school system.

I noticed that the public school system was heavily influenced by the government, the WHO, corporations, big pharma, and others. Why do many teachers praise the medical system and the mainstream media medical opinions on COVID? Teachers deem them reliable and tell students to trust them because they would never lie and risk their reputation. When it comes to alternative news sources or supposedly discredited doctors, teachers say they are lying and call them crazy anti-maskers, anti-vaxxers, or conspiracy theorists.

I really think that most teachers have good intentions and go into teaching because they just want to help and make a positive difference in the lives of young people. Sadly, many teachers seem completely unaware that they are indoctrinating students with propaganda and agendas that benefit and serve the interests of big corporations and the media.

I find it very interesting that schools are disseminating social justice politics, LGBTQ, gender politics, critical race theory, climate alarmism, UN Agenda 2030, and public health fear mongering in Socials, English and Science classes. These topics were always presented as fact, with no room for individual opinions or critical debate. I believe that it is being repeated as a brainwashing technique. Here are some examples:

In English classes, we had to read one awful science fiction, dystopian, futuristic novel after another -- futures where people lived in virtual online worlds, and where humans would fight each other for food and survival. This was so disturbing to me. I can certainly see the connections between these stories and some of the scenarios happening now.

In science classes, we were inundated with information about past pandemics and viruses – SARS, measles, swine flu, H1N1, and that vaccines are the only cure to save lives. I came home in Grade 8 terrified that I would get polio until my mom calmed me down and reassured me.

As the year went on, I noticed how quickly they added COVID brainwashing to the learning curriculum. Teachers would go over COVID protocol and fear mongered about COVID whenever we started a new class.

COVID propaganda as well as Bonnie Henry quotes were plastered all over the wall: Wear a mask, sanitize, social distance, be kind, be calm, be safe, be a good human being, do your part and keep everyone safe. I countered these by putting up stickers in the girls' bathroom that I got from rallies.

Teachers and students were proud of their vaccines and masks, and they wanted to broadcast a virtue signal to everyone that they were vaccinated and wearing masks.

In June 2021, my Grade 12 science class teacher gave me an assignment to write and present a short paper about how the COVID vaccines work and their benefits. That just crossed the line for me. I was so upset when I received this assignment. I wasn't going to tell the teacher what he wanted to hear. I was going to tell what I think is the truth. I created a well-sourced paper with reasons not to get the vaccine, with some help from my mom.

I presented my arguments to my class. Afterwards I posted my paper on my science Google Classroom page so everyone could read it. I am really hoping that what I did made some of my classmates and my teacher think about and question what we are being told.

Near the end of the school year, the school emailed the students a COVID vaccine survey from BC Children's Hospital. The survey asked about student vaccine status and plans for vaccination. It stated the answers to the survey would be anonymous, though if the student gave their email address they would get a one hour volunteer certificate and their contact info would be collected. My mom wasn't notified of this survey. They went behind the parents' backs. I wonder if this was their way to check to see if teens are supportive of mandatory vaccines.

When the vaccines came out, I was so concerned that I texted all my friend contacts with a message to say that this is an experimental vaccine. I also sent along videos from doctors. Most ignored the message and a few replied that they would be going to get it anyway. I was happy to hear two people say they weren't going to get it. So, there are others not in support of the current agenda. And I believe there are more of us.

Parents need to ask, "Why are these agendas being incorporated into the public school curriculum, and can students recognize that they are being brainwashed?"

The Future of Learning

I believe that the school indoctrination is only going to get worse and will be added to the lower grade learning curriculum. Recently I met a retired kindergarten teacher who told me the public school curriculum wanted her to teach kindergarteners transgender ideology, to tell them it's okay to want to be another gender, and to not refer to them as boys and girls but instead by pronouns 'he', 'she', 'they', and 'them'.

The public education system needs to be critically examined and drastically overhauled. The UN, WHO, big corporations and pharma, and government influence have no place in school curriculums. The indoctrination has got to stop. Until then, parents should consider homeschooling their children and letting their school administrators know why they are removing their children from the system.

Hope and Inspiring Young People

When more people stop complying and giving the rest of the crowd the illusion of consensus, perhaps maybe around 10% or more of us, this will give permission to those around us to doubt what's going on. We need to be the noisy 10%!

This terrible situation we're in is only able to carry on because people are conforming.

This tyranny could not go on if people simply stopped doing what they are told. If more of us could show, with our behaviour and actions, that we are not in agreement, that could break the spell!

What I've learned so far is that standing alone is psychologically painful. Sometimes you just have to do it!

Stand in your own truth.

Know your rights.

Be willing to stand in your power.

Let your voice be counted.

I've come to realize there's no one coming to save us. "We ARE the ones we've been waiting for!" I know it's not easy, but try to stay positive and in the light. We are going to share the truth and get through this.

Love,

Callie Ocean

About Callie Ocean:

Callie grew up in Squamish, BC and attended the Waldorf school there through Grade 4. She attended public school in Squamish, until moving to West Vancouver and attending West Vancouver Senior Secondary (WVSS) for Grade 10 in 2019, graduating a year early in June 2021.

She was an avid horseback rider and gymnast, and she also took acting and dance classes prior to the pandemic. When COVID hit, her extracurricular activities ended. Recently she has taken up voice lessons and kickboxing.

Since graduating, she plans to sing, follow her heart, and be a free, unvaccinated human!

Chapter Eighteen

The Doctors

By Dr. Stephen Malthouse

The COVID propaganda war is still on. Only a handful of Canadian doctors have taken up arms to battle the government, public health, and the medical colleges, not to mention colleagues who believe that speaking out against Theresa Tam, Bonnie Henry, and similar public health experts (*read:* Canadian criminals) is tantamount to murder through the spread of misinformation. The outspoken doctors are all under investigation and threat by their provincial colleges and it's likely that each college has a stack of complaint letters that we don't even know about. Yet.

In the last hundred years, the world's medical profession has been put under a spell. That spell was cast by a sophisticated program leading us to trust everything that Big Pharma dictated through our peer-reviewed journals, medical media, and institutions. We are a captured profession and, like most hypnotized subjects, will vehemently deny that we have gone under. The trance was necessary for the current horrors of the fake pandemic to be rolled out without medical opposition. Because of our knowledge and the public's trust in doctors, physicians represented the greatest threat to the Great Reset and could not be allowed to remain awake. It has been a long, intentional process.

Miraculously, several Canadian doctors broke that spell last year:

Dr. Kulvinder Gill Kaur has been a staunch defender of early treatments such as hydroxychloroquine for COVID. She was viciously attacked by colleagues and the Ontario College for her advocacy of early treatment on her social media.

Dr. Mark Trozzi resigned from emergency medicine, where his questioning of the COVID scam began ruffling feathers and became a prolific journalist chronicling every sinister piece of the agenda as it rolled out.

Dr. Patrick Phillips continues rural emergency medicine in Ontario and has spoken frequently about the harms of COVID public health measures, such as lockdowns, masks, and the gene-modifying injections on his patients. He spoke on Parliament Hill about the censoring of doctors who have concerns about the mainstream COVID narrative.

Dr. Jeff Matheson had his license suspended in Ontario for raising concerns about absurd public health policies.

Dr. Neda Amani lost her 15-year contract with the Ottawa police force when she became a political pariah for speaking out boldly.

Dr. Charles Hoffe lost his job after identifying a flurry of neurologic injuries in his patients after the COVID vaxx and relaying his observations to his regional public health officer. The doctor in charge of adverse event reporting in BC informed Dr. Hoffe that his patients' injuries were just a "coincidence".

Saskatchewan surgeon, Dr. Francis Christian, was invited to a Star Chamber "interview" where he was stripped of his teaching privileges because he dared to suggest the need for informed consent before injecting twelve-to-seventeen-year-olds with an experimental COVID vaccine. Dr. Christian knew he was "on the right side of history" and, when his accusers suggested he might need psychological support (a Canadian gulag, perhaps?), he assured them that it was they who would need psychiatric help when their crimes against humanity were revealed. As for himself, he "slept well at night", having followed his conscience. Other doctors have stepped up to the plate: Dr. Bill Code, Dr. Dorle Kneifel, Dr. Caroline Turek, Dr. Keren Epstein-Gilboa, Dr. Biz Bastian, Dr. Chris Milburn, Dr. Jean Marc Benoit, Dr. Roger Hodkinson, Dr. Matt Strauss, and more.

I, myself, am a reluctant warrior. After 42 years of practicing medicine, most recently in rural family practice, I decided to take a sabbatical in January 2020 and pursue meditation training. Things didn't work out quite the way I had planned.

In Spring 2020, when we still thought that COVID was going to be a tsunami of death and destruction, Canadian doctors tried to get prepared. We were scared. There were stories of physicians changing their clothes in the garage when returning home, so as not to infect their families. We heard of Chinese hospitals filled with intubated COVID patients, most of them dying. Then there were the body bags lined up on the sidewalks and Chinese pedestrians (a few bad actors, it turns out) dropping dead in the street. We desperately needed effective therapies.

In March, I sent my first letter to the BC provincial health officer, Dr. Bonnie Henry, presenting research that supported the use of vitamin D supplements for respiratory illnesses in the elderly. I also reached out to our local hospital medical director, provincial Long Term Care supervisors, and Indigenous Health authorities. No one seemed at all interested in either vitamin D or vitamin C, despite the evidence. A phone call revealed that our hospital pharmacy did not even stock intravenous vitamin C, the only in-hospital therapy working in China at the time. I became involved in research with the American Institute of Homeopathy, where remedies used successfully in COVID cases were recorded and the data distributed to practitioners. A Chinese doctor was prescribing homeopathy at the Hong Kong airport to new arrivals, many of them returning students, and had also successfully treated an enormous number of people in Macau. The remedies Bryonia, Gelsemium, Arsenicum, and Phosphorus appeared at the top of the effective medication list. Using that information, I created a preventive treatment program for Denman Island, where I live, and offered it to frontline workers and elderly patients. News of hydroxychloroquine was just beginning to break into the medical literature.

In May 2020, the Canadian Integrative Medicine Association, of which I was the president, composed a statement outlining all the known measures, including intravenous vitamin C, selenium, vitamin D3, and zinc, which could be used to combat COVID-19. We imagined the authorities would be enthusiastic. Yet, despite hiring a media relations firm to spread the word, no one in the mainstream media got back to us. Meanwhile, my local doctors' bulletin board was ignoring any discussion of preventive therapies, concentrating on the acquisition of personal protective equipment (PPE), and getting the right forms in order. Nobody seemed the least bit interested in hydroxychloroquine and emerging treatment research. Everyone was keeping busy but not actually seeing COVID patients. Doctors were leaving their clinics to practice telehealth, which was considered safer for them.

Meanwhile, the hospitals remained empty of COVID cases. The emergency rooms were vacant, the ICUs far short of capacity. During this time, the mainstream media continued to describe a wave of death that did not really exist in BC. Our chief provincial health officer, Dr. Bonnie Henry, was now receiving accolades for beating back the pandemic onslaught and an adoring media-led public began to herald her as a saviour. A shoe designer in Vancouver created an expensive new style and named it after her. The New York Times ran a photograph of her communing with God through a stained glass window and proclaimed her to be a Canadian saint. Royal Roads University in Victoria bestowed her an honorary law degree.

A few of us were now scratching our heads and wondering what was going on.

After making some simple calculations and listening to the epidemiologists, we concluded that this was not really a pandemic after all, but more like a typical flu season. The narrative of constant invisible viral danger that was being broadcast over millions of TV sets around the world by “experts” (a story swallowed whole by the majority of the medical profession) did not match what was happening on the ground. Unbelievably, it seemed that our leaders were terrorizing the Canadian public with a propaganda campaign. In fact, this same fear-mongering and populace control was being instigated globally.

In June, I organized some local gatherings to discuss the flurry of confusing public health policies under which we were then labouring. This generated a few complaints from fellow Denman Islanders to BC’s medical College, accusing me of disseminating misinformation. Frivolous complaints by anxious islanders began to accumulate on the Registrar’s desk every time I wrote something in the local Grapevine newspaper. After all these years, I was finally developing a reputation. Having been the main family doctor on Denman Island for the preceding 13 years, several of these accusations came from my old patients.

Then came masking in Summer 2020, an absurd practice that could not stop an aerosolized 0.1 µm sized virus. Nevertheless, Dr. Bonnie Henry in British Columbia continued to recommend face coverings, standing 6 feet apart (the distance one can spit), and staying indoors to combat a virus that was no longer present in our community. Asymptomatic people, for the first time in history and independent of any research, were convinced by the propaganda machine that they were killers and that no grandmother was safe. Long-term care homes locked their doors, preventing visitors who might unknowingly be harbouring the deadly virus. The frail elderly were made prisoners and were detained in solitary confinement. Parks were closed, schools were closed, businesses were closed. An attempt was made to close down human life. The world was led in "only-two-weeks-more" policy increments towards a state of abject fear and willingness to obey. The unraveling of society had begun and both our elected government and appointed public health experts continued to implement measures of destruction. In retrospect, there can be no doubt that this was intentional.

In October 2020, I wrote an open letter to Dr. Bonnie Henry, challenging her policies and pointing out her mismanagement of the so-called pandemic. None of my colleagues were willing to co-sign this letter with me for fear of retribution. One psychiatrist colleague told me I was angry, and the letter was too harsh. After all, Bonnie Henry was just doing her job. Other colleagues thought an appeasing personal letter would be more professional. I was surprised at how little my integrative medicine colleagues were willing to back me up. Perhaps they just didn't see what was happening before their very eyes. Or they calculated that the personal risk was too great.

My open letter concluded with:

> "The mainstream media has created a religion out of public health, one based on superstition, not science, with the power to rule over an obedient public. The news channels have raised you [Bonnie Henry] to almost saint-like status. Tea towels, shoes, and murals have been designed to celebrate your accomplishments. Yet, your public directives do not make sense. They contradict the research, and they are causing people a great deal of harm. As a fellow doctor, I appeal to you to re-examine your policies and change direction before Public Health causes irreparable damage to our province's health and economic well-being. That about-face will require you to meet the obligations of your office."

Well, you can imagine how well that went over at the BC College of Physicians and Surgeons. As soon as the open letter hit social media, the College called me with an invitation to attend a preliminary interview, but it was clear that a full investigation was underway. Now I had begun to notice something peculiar about the Canadian Medical Protective Association upon which all doctors rely for legal representation: their lawyers appeared to know all the first names of the secretaries at the College and have a cozy relationship with them. I began to have an uneasy feeling that I was going to be walked out over the quicksand in my upcoming interview with the College registrar. So, in their place, I hired Rocco Galati, a well-known constitutional lawyer with real teeth that he had been known to use on occasion. My first (and only) interview lasted about 10 minutes when the College stubbornly refused to record the meeting, had a brief scuffle with Rocco, lost a few fingers in the fight (psychologically speaking), and retired from the field of battle. (Subsequently, I have heard that the College's notes and recall often contain inaccuracies that the physician under investigation is no longer in a position to refute.)

That was the beginning of my infamous career of speaking out publicly against the COVID *plandemic*. Since then, I have been interviewed on numerous occasions and spoken at rallies in Vancouver, Kelowna, and up and down Vancouver Island. There is no denying that people are getting sick and dying from COVID, but statistics do not support a real pandemic and the mortality to date has been similar to a bad flu season. Even that could have been prevented to a large degree by vitamin D supplementation, hydroxychloroquine/zinc/azithromycin or ivermectin, the use of which are all still discouraged by Health Canada and most hospitals. The real deadly agents are turning out to be our public health experts and the governments behind them. Of course, the CDC and the WHO are being *them*. Like a Russian Matryoshka doll, one can keep going deeper to find more and more elite criminals. At the moment, the public is being coerced into taking fake COVID vaccines that nobody needs and almost certainly contain nanotechnology with gene-modifying capabilities designed to alter the genetics of humanity. We have entered a sci-fi scenario that no one believed was possible.

The question we are all asking ourselves, when trying to understand the *plandemic* psychology and the varied susceptibility to hypnosis, is how did some people escape the programming? Then what made those escapees stand up and speak to Power? Those are questions that we seem unable to answer. It doesn't seem related to how many credentials you have after your name. Intelligence doesn't seem to matter. In fact, it could be a liability if you have a prestigious well-paying position at a university where conformity, group-think, and coercion from directors are more likely. Is good heartedness a determinant? Nope. The Dalai Lama publicly took the shot (which probably means he is not in on the hoax).

But we have figured out that those doctors speaking to Power today are not here by accident. When we trace our careers, it is clear that everything led to this point where we are fully prepared for battle. We have the skills, we are in the right place, we have the personal experience, we are motivated. As for myself, I began practicing medicine in 1978, after which I did locums for 11 years, never quite finding conventional medicine satisfying. I trained in homeopathy and married a naturopath. I spent a year and a half in meditation retreat and then two years overseas in Kathmandu, doing medical research and studying Buddhism. I've had extra training in palliative care, and in emergency and rural medicine. I studied acupuncture and have a keen interest in orthomolecular medicine and nutrition. I've heard Norman Cousins and Linus Pauling speak. I take vitamins. I've been involved in founding several integrative and complementary medicine associations. And my story is not unusual among the doctors now standing up and risking persecution by their colleges, approbation by their colleagues, and even the censure of their communities.

The Colleges of Physicians and Surgeons of Ontario and British Columbia both came out with statements forbidding doctors in their provinces from speaking out against wearing masks, social distancing, lockdowns, and COVID "vaccination". But, as physicians, we chose to put people first, not public health policy, college degrees, or popular opinion, and we are willing to lose our medical licenses on behalf of human rights and freedoms. That fight is now a necessity as our profession, in fact the whole world, is in the hands of the pill purveyors, i.e. the pharmaceutical industry and their overlords. This will change. While conventional medicine has its strength in treating emergencies, where rapid stabilization is essential, and in surgery when medical means are unsuccessful, orthodox medicine is an abysmal failure in treating chronic disease. The Rockefellers captured the medical profession around 1900, with the Flexner report and a lot of petroleum money. They and their cronies began dictating the curricula of the medical schools and buying the names of experts to apply to ghostwritten articles in "peer-reviewed" journals. In this way, Big Pharma was born, and Germ Theory ascended to the throne. Now a tiny virus is being used as an excuse for a global takeover by technocrats.

Something spectacular is coming. We have pulled back the curtain and seen the culprits who are manipulating the levers. If the pandemic has given us anything, it is the opportunity to see the manipulation behind the scenes. And once the full extent of that deceit has been revealed, and this applies especially to the practice of medicine and its institutions, it cannot be hidden away behind the curtain again. When we replace the old systems and paradigms, we will need to safeguard against this same level of corruption occurring again, and that can only be achieved by a significant change in human nature: a change that will distinguish man from AI and machines. That will only occur with an increase in self-awareness and the awakening of conscience, the two essential qualities that allow us to fearlessly stand up with integrity and speak to Power.

About Dr. Stephen Malthouse:

Dr. Stephen Malthouse is a physician in British Columbia, Canada, and the current president of both the Canadian Integrative Medicine Association and the Canada Health Alliance (CHA). The CHA is an umbrella organization of doctors, nurses, chiropractors, naturopaths, and other healthcare practitioners who have a vision for improving the future well-being of Canadians. Dr. Malthouse has been practicing medicine since 1978 in rural, urban, emergency room, palliative care, and family practice settings and was involved in overseas research into childhood illness while living in Kathmandu, Nepal for two years. He has a special interest in integrative medicine, which uses both conventional and alternative therapies in day-to-day medical practice. Dr. Malthouse started a sabbatical year in 2020 and inadvertently began studying COVID-19 research and the Canadian government and public health responses to a so-called "pandemic" of their own making. One of Canada's first doctors to speak out against the government's pandemic policies, he is best known for writing an open letter to the BC Chief Public Health Officer advising her to reverse policies that were causing individual and societal damage that could last for generations. He continues to be a vocal critic of the government's management of the COVID crisis, which itself appears to be a cover story for a clandestine attempt at creating a global technocracy.

Chapter Nineteen

Voice of Truth

By Kristal Nicole Pitter

In John 8:32, Jesus said, "Then you will know the truth, and the truth will set you free."

For as long as I can remember, I have been a truth seeker and speaker who is dedicated to lifelong learning both personally and professionally. I adhere to a code of ethics that is unshakable and requires that I do unto others as I would have them do unto me. I'm extremely passionate about speaking, advocating, standing strong for truth and all that is noble, and opposing and exposing deceit, corruption, and evil. I'm a deeply compassionate person and professional who is dedicated to the safety and health of humanity. I have always strived to do everything possible to empower patients to take charge of their own health and achieve the best possible outcomes. Because I love others, I must speak the truth.

It was a blessing to grow up in a Christian environment where the family not only shared the gospel of Jesus Christ but also demonstrated His love in tangible ways. My steadfast faith in God has anchored me in peace and hope even when faced with adversity, uncertainty, heartache, and pain. Religion is dead, dry, ritualistic, legalistic, and powerless, but I can attest that a personal relationship with my Lord and Savior is alive, exciting, living, breathing, and filled with Holy Spirit power that brings restoration, healing, deliverance from bondage, and freedom from captivity. My faith has empowered me to overcome difficult trials in my life that were instrumental in shaping me into the tenacious warrior I've become today.

Acclimatizing to the separation and divorce of my parents at a very young age was a significantly traumatic experience. My entire world crumbled. Like many kids, I somehow felt responsible and endeavored to do everything in my power to repair the fracture in our family. But, as the nursery rhyme goes, I couldn't put my family back together again. Spirits of rejection and abandonment were waiting to pounce.

In 1 Peter 5:8, we are told to "Be sober, be vigilant, because your enemy, the devil, prowls around like a roaring lion looking for someone to devour." The thief comes to steal, kill, and destroy. (John 10:10) He is a liar who whispered deception into my ear repeatedly for years, causing me to question my value and identity. I craved unconditional love and acceptance, which led to unhealthy and destructive coping mechanisms. I became a performing monkey that was focused on people pleasing, striving for perfection, and naively believing I could control situations to prevent myself from being hurt, while earning the love and acceptance I so desperately wanted and needed. I became an overachiever in academics, sports, and in all areas where I applied myself, earning certificates, degrees, ribbons, trophies, and other awards. These achievements ultimately left me feeling empty.

Like so many others, I began to look for love in all the wrong places. I dated my high school sweetheart for seven years, believing one day I would marry him, only to find myself heartbroken as I gazed out a city bus window on my way to university one morning, watching him embrace another girl on the sidewalk.

Betrayal. It cuts like a knife, causing deep and painful wounds that leave ugly scars. Instantaneously, feelings of rejection and abandonment came flooding back. I spiraled into a state of depression. I moved back home with my parents after finishing my first year of university and withdrew from everyone and everything. I rarely left my bedroom, emerging mainly to report to work as a waitress and to eat. Many nights I cried myself to sleep, asking God to pull me out of that deep pit of despair.

I knew that only God could take my shattered heart and make it beat again. He showed me that a heart planted in forgiveness doesn't dwell in the past, that my identity and value are found in Him alone, and that I needed to start *living* again, not merely existing. I needed to trust God with my future.

Then one warm night that summer, I stepped out in faith and took my youngest brother to our town fair. Everything changed in a moment. I met the amazing man that four years later would become my husband. Having experienced both betrayal and heartache, there was an instantaneous and meaningful connection. The intersection of our lives was divinely orchestrated. God is never early or late. His timing is always perfect. We must learn to be patient. Everything in our lives happens for a reason. There are no coincidences.

My decision to become a nurse evolved out of the belief that nursing was a vocation that provided opportunities to make a palpable and positive difference in the lives of others at times when they are not only facing health-related challenges but also at their most vulnerable. Many family members pursued professions in health care, including my mother, father, grandmother, and aunt. Their selfless dedication to caring, protecting, and advocating for others inspired me to follow the example they role modeled. I desired to protect and serve the public by ensuring safe and ethical care.

Completing the Primary Health Care Nurse Practitioner Program at a time when my daughters were 5 and 4 years of age was a grueling experience. It was an intense and exhausting period of time consumed with studying, exams, essay submissions, and clinical placements. Most days I was sleep-deprived and on an emotional roller coaster. I kept reminding myself that "this too shall pass" and "all the hard work will be rewarded." My husband was and continues to be by my side every step of the way, loving, encouraging, and supporting me, through good times and adversity. My heart overflows with gratitude when I reflect on how much I appreciate having him on this life journey with me. Thankfully, our parents provided their assistance on numerous occasions during this challenging period. I'm abundantly blessed to have such a loving and generous family.

I received approximately half a day of training on immunizations during the course of my education. We were provided with the Ontario Immunization Schedule, instructed regarding which vaccines to give and when, advised that vaccines are safe and effective, and were led to believe they are required to protect against disease. This concerned me, given that our Creator masterfully created our bodies with a magnificent immune system. A healthy diet, exercise, adequate hydration and sleep, reduced stress, fresh air, sun exposure, and vitamin and mineral supplements such as vitamins C, D, and zinc help to protect and enhance our immune system. Sadly, these are not being discussed or addressed by Public Health.

In my role as a Nurse Practitioner, I became aware of Dr. William Thompson, senior scientist at the Centers for Disease Control and Prevention (CDC). In 2014, Dr. Thompson came forward as a whistleblower to expose alleged scientific fraud that occurred between 2000 and 2004. Dr. Thompson noted a documented increase in autism rates in male African American children if they received the MMR vaccine on time according to the CDC vaccination schedule. This information disturbed me greatly, prompting me to take a deep dive into vaccines. I watched documentaries including *Vaxxed: From Cover-Up to Catastrophe*; *Vaxxed II: The People's Truth*; *Trace Amounts;* and *1986: The Act*. These films awakened me to the truth about vaccines. I discovered an extensive list of harmful and unethical ingredients and adjuvants contained in vaccines, including aluminum, mercury/thimerosal, polysorbate 80, formaldehyde, aborted fetal cells, and animal DNA, just to name a few. I was appalled to learn that manufacturers are completely immune to all liability.

As time passed, I became greatly concerned about the medical tyranny I was witnessing in my practice. I was directed by management not to inform my patients that life begins at conception. It was acceptable to discuss risks of pregnancy but forbidden to discuss risks associated with abortion. Omissions are as untruthful as misinformation. Suddenly, I found myself in the midst of a system I didn't recognize or appreciate anymore -- a system that violated the very standards to which we are mandated to adhere. A significant nursing role is to ensure that patients are provided with all available high-level medical and scientific evidence to inform decision-making and consent.

It became apparent the medical industry wasn't what I believed it was. Health care is really sick care. Medications are prescribed as a band-aid approach that usually requires additional pharmaceuticals to manage the side effects of the original medication prescribed. Many have been indoctrinated to believe that health only comes in the form of a pill or needle. Of course, this provides a very lucrative business for Big Pharma as lifelong customers return through the perpetual revolving door. My philosophy is that a holistic approach to health promotion and illness prevention is required that incorporates the entire person -- body, soul (mind, will, emotions), and spirit into care. True healing is focused on identifying the root cause of illness rather than symptom management.

"A cheerful heart is good medicine, but a crushed spirit dries up the bones." ~ Proverbs 17:22 ~

When the *plandemic* was declared, I knew almost immediately that something was amiss. The implementation of mask use to prevent viral transmission was a major red flag. Viruses are approximately 0.1 microns in size, much smaller than the pores of a mask. Trying to prevent viral transmission by mask wearing is like trying to prevent mosquitoes from travelling through a chain link fence. Ninety-nine percent of viral particles are airborne, entering the eyes and skin pores in addition to the mouth and nose. Masks deplete the body of necessary oxygen for proper functioning of each cell and lead to an increase in carbon dioxide levels. No one would ever occlude the exhaust of a car and allow toxic poisons to build up within the vehicle. Likewise, exhaled carbon dioxide should never be trapped in a mask, forcing us to rebreathe the waste materials our lungs are designed to expel. This leads to an acidic pH, increased cortisol levels due to being in a state of stress, and a compromised immune system. Masks also trap heat and moisture. A warm and moist environment is the perfect medium for growth and multiplication of harmful bacteria and fungi leading to increased risk of dental caries, mask mouth, infections such as impetigo, and bacterial pneumonia, among other health concerns. Heat and moisture can also cause the wearer to inhale chemicals and fibers from the mask.

In 2015 and 2018, a grievance and arbitration process initiated by the Ontario Nurses Association challenged health care employers to present and provide evidence-based research that demonstrated that wearing masks and getting influenza vaccines prevented the transmission of influenza in health care settings. Health employers presented scientific research and used expert witnesses, including Dr. Bonnie Henry, British Columbia Provincial Health Officer, to discuss the scientific research and evidence in support of masking policies in Ontario health care settings. The arbitrators in both cases concluded that there was inadequate scientific evidence and research to support that mask use and flu vaccines prevented the transmission of influenza. Health employers' policies were struck down as a result, setting a precedent. This knowledge confirmed that the actions taken in response to COVID-19 required further research.

To confirm my knowledge, I examined the masking evidence from many sources including *Masks Don't Work: A review of science relevant to COVID-19 social policy*, completed by Denis G. Rancourt, PhD, Ontario Civil Liberties Association Researcher; a video entitled *Masks Exposed and the Health Risks Involved* with Tammy Clark and Kristen Meghan, Occupational Safety and Health Administration (OSHA) experts in the USA; and a pamphlet entitled *Masks for COVID-19?* developed by Chris Schaefer, Edmonton Respirator Expert.

The science hasn't changed. It is well known that masks are ineffective in the prevention of viral transmission. Far worse, masks are dangerous. There is absolutely no evidence to validate mask wearing, social distancing, PCR testing, lockdowns, and the closure of school, church, and small business.

Truth be known, masks are a symbol of submission. They are dehumanizing, stealing our breath and voice. Masks are a strategic tool utilized to enslave humanity. It's time to courageously stand in opposition to government corruption, expose medical fraud, and hold our leaders accountable for their actions. This is only a very small part of a demonic agenda planned long ago to usher in a New World Order (NWO). The Georgia Guidestones clearly indicate the NWO agenda is depopulation and reproduction control to maintain a global population under 500 million.

It is well known that collateral damage from COVID-19 measures is causing more harm and destruction. We are seeing alarming rates of depression, anxiety, isolation, alcoholism, self-harm, suicide, domestic abuse, overdose, cancer and cardiac deaths, unemployment, homelessness, business closures and bankruptcies, destruction of the economy, and poverty. Those who need access to necessary and emergent health care should never be turned away or have appointments, assessments, or surgeries delayed or cancelled. The damage being done to mental health due to isolation and harmful messaging is devastating. Our children should not be taught they are vectors of disease that could be responsible for killing Grandma.

When harmful measures lacking medical and scientific evidence were implemented in response to COVID-19, I embraced the role of whistleblower by boldly and courageously speaking truth on social media to protect the health and safety of humanity, despite the risk of opposition and retribution. I cannot and will not remain silent when I know that the measures imposed are not supported by evidence, and that they cause more harm to society. My moral and ethical codes demand that I speak the truth and advocate for the public. I must stand with integrity and righteousness. I will not violate my conscience. I refuse to bow to man. No opposition could ever prevent me from doing the right thing. My life belongs to Jesus. I surrender all that I have and all that I am. I have been called to be the hands and feet of Jesus to everyone I encounter, and the salt and light in a dark and hurting world. I was born for such a time as this!

Media outlets published defamatory articles in relation to my social media posts in July 2020. I was falsely portrayed as a selfish person, a danger to society, a conspiracy theorist, and many demanded that my license to practice nursing be revoked. I was investigated by both my employer and the College of Nurses of Ontario. I was terminated from my job and my license is being threatened. I was viciously attacked online. It was extremely hurtful to experience such vitriol, but I will not be derailed from my assignment. Thank God I've overcome rejection. It's painful to witness family, friends, and colleagues turn their back on you, completely unaware that you are speaking truth and fighting to protect their health and future. The love, support, encouragement, and new relationships that have been established far outweigh any losses. I pray everyone has eyes to see, ears to hear, and hearts and spirits that are sensitive to receive the truth before it's too late.

Everyone must do all they can to help others understand what is really happening and why. This has nothing to do with health. We are dealing with a nefarious politicized agenda that is all about fear, control, profit, and genocide. The evidence is easily attained by researching the World Economic Forum, Davos, The Rockefeller Foundation, The Bill and Melinda Gates Foundation, Event 201, Agenda 21, and Agenda 2030. Discernment is paramount. This is a war between good and evil. We are fighting a spiritual battle. *Now* is the time to get engaged and impact your sphere of influence. Make new connections and share truth with everyone. We each have a vital role to play. Be strong and courageously stand in opposition to fear and control. Stop complying. Choose to stand on the right side of history. Our ancestors fought and died for our freedoms, and we *must* do the same. Be *brave*. Rise up against tyrannical totalitarianism and communism and take back our lives, country, and freedom. Our children, grandchildren, and future generations are depending on us.

COVID-19 taught us a very valuable lesson. When led through a fire, there's a reason for the flames. We have been given an opportunity to repent and turn back to God. Only God can bring beauty from the depths of our pain. We have been distracted and in pursuit of worldly things and pleasures. It's time for a reset, but *not* the Great Reset and the UN Sustainable Development Goals. We need to reset our priorities and our lives to focus on what is most important: faith, family, freedom, community, and health. God of mercy and love, we pray that You expose all the deceit, corruption, fraud, and crimes against humanity. Do what only You can do and make all things new. You can make a way where there seems to be no way.

We are about to experience the greatest revival and awakening the world has ever seen as God pours out His Spirit on all flesh. God's mighty hand of justice will prevail, and He alone will receive all glory, honour, praise, and worship!

In closing, I would like to share a few scriptures and quotations that have been extremely encouraging:

"There is no fear in love, but perfect love casts out fear." ~ 1 John 4:18 ~

"For God has not given us a spirit of fear, but of power, of love, and of a sound mind." ~ 2 Timothy 1:7 ~

"For there is nothing hidden that will not be disclosed, and nothing concealed that will not be made known and brought to light." ~ Luke 8:17 ~

"For we wrestle not against flesh and blood, but against principalities, against powers, against the rulers of the darkness of this world, against spiritual wickedness in high places." ~ Ephesians 6:12 ~

"A lie doesn't become truth, wrong doesn't become right, and evil doesn't become good, just because it's accepted by a majority." ~ Booker T. Washington ~

"Silence in the face of evil is itself evil. God will not hold us guiltless. Not to speak is to speak. Not to act is to act." ~ Dietrich Bonhoeffer ~

I dedicate this chapter first and foremost to my Lord and Savior Jesus Christ; my husband Craig; my daughters Nicole and Rachel; my parents, Rick, Jeannie, Rita, and Dale; my grandmother Madeline; and my auntie Kim. Thank you for all your love, support, encouragement, and prayers throughout my life. You have all been instrumental over the years, each having a vital role in assisting me to become a relentless warrior who advocates for truth, freedom, and justice.

About Kristal Nicole Pitter:

Kristal was born and raised in Tillsonburg, a small town in southwestern Ontario. She is married to her husband, Craig; is mother to two beautiful daughters, Nicole and Rachel; and she is sister to two younger brothers. Kristal is very honoured and privileged to be a member of the Canadian Frontline Nurses, Canada Health Alliance, and Vaccine Choice Canada, and to be included in *The Brave 2: Speaking Truth to Power.*

Kristal began her nursing journey by obtaining her Registered Nursing Diploma (RN) from Conestoga College of Applied Arts and Technology in 1996. She pursued further studies, obtaining her Bachelor of Science in Nursing Degree (BScN) from the University of Western Ontario in 2000 and graduated with distinction from the University of Western Ontario with a certificate as a Primary Health Care Nurse Practitioner (PHCNP) in 2007. Kristal has been practicing nursing for 24 years in the areas of medicine/surgery, community, geriatrics, obstetrics/gynecology, paramedical services, public health, maternal/child health, sexual health, infectious disease, primary health care, management, and long-term care home inspection.

Kristal is passionately committed to ending the injustice of abortion, the leading cause of death in the world. She is a powerful voice for the voiceless, promoting respect for all unborn children and protecting the sanctity of life from conception to natural death.

When harmful measures lacking medical and scientific evidence were implemented in response to COVID-19, Kristal embraced the role of whistleblower when she boldly and courageously spoke truth to protect the health and safety of humanity, despite the risk of reprisal.

www.canadianfrontlinenurses.ca

Chapter Twenty

The Logical Choice

By RC The Rapper

On With The Show

As one of the few musicians going against the grain, a lot of people ask me what inspired me to do what I do. For that, we have to go all the way back to the beginning, circa the mid-2000s.

After a friend and I smoked a joint, he started trying to convince me that the Twin Towers were brought down by controlled demolition and that George Bush was in on it. He told me to check some stuff out. I told him he was an idiot and I would debunk it and get back to him. I stuck to my word and promptly set out to prove him wrong. But to my surprise and wonder, I quickly realized I couldn't, and found my skeptical mind shifting its focus from the "conspiracies" to the official narrative. The more I learned, the stranger the reality. There were things about the event that could not be explained away within the framework of the story we were told. I uncovered facts that outright refuted the official narrative, and thus my world was changed forever.

How could it be? Right in front of my eyes, an entire piece of history was fabricated. The only logical explanations involved corruption and malice at the highest levels, and a conspiracy so grand it put every Hollywood script to shame.

The news that we trusted to keep us informed was actively trying to deceive us.

It is not possible for two planes to pulverize three buildings into piles of dust. The idea is laughable in any other context. The collapse of the third building, WTC7, is so unexplainable that the 9/11 commission report (the "official investigation") *did not even mention it* following a two year "investigation." Yet with zero evidence or even an argument that makes sense based on what we can see with our eyes, one must admire the mainstream's audacity in their bold-faced and unwavering assurance that two planes did indeed pulverize three buildings.

As Joseph Goebbels, the Nazi propagandist once said, "If you tell a lie big enough and keep repeating it often enough, the people will come to believe it." Our own "democratic" media was taking a page directly out of the socialist playbook, but the scariest part of all is that normal, otherwise intelligent people were starting to repeat the lies. It was surreal to watch people try to explain falsehoods. Office fires cannot cause a building to collapse at freefall speed. Not in this universe, anyway. The "official explanation" defied physics and betrayed our eyes, yet nobody seemed to notice.

This sent me on a path of questioning everything and into a period of researching as much as possible about the forces that shape our world. From then on, I refused to allow anyone else to think for me. I learned about the Bohemian Grove and the Finders Cult, the Gulf of Tonkin and Operation Paperclip. I learned about the history of fractional reserve banking and the Federal Reserve Act. I learned about families that had been wealthy and influential for centuries but somehow managed to stay out of the history books. I learned who owns the media and Hollywood.

I've learned a great deal, and I continue to learn all the time. Since my re-education, I've kept a very open mind.

We live in a very rich tapestry, and truth is stranger than fiction.

The full extent is far beyond the scope of this chapter, but what I would uncover in the following years led me to realize that the only framework in which the world made sense was that of a grand conspiracy, the end game of which was the enslavement of the entire human race by a small cult who had been working towards their goal for centuries. Sounds crazy, right? But much of this concept is not a secret, and anyone who performs an honest assessment of modern history can only reach the same conclusion. The same handful of inbreeding families have dominated the main levers of power all over the globe since before the industrial revolution. The governments of the world are their tools, and neither this ruling class nor the governments they command care about the masses despite the façade. If they did, the world would not be the way it is. America spends hundreds of billions of dollars per year on military expansion but can't seem to solve the homelessness in Los Angeles. This is not how benevolent rulers behave.

I learned that this "elite" cult was closer than ever to their goals, and much of the necessary infrastructure was already in place. This does not necessarily mean they will be totally successful with their attempt. I always believed in the wild card that is the spirit of humanity. But it meant at some point in my lifetime I would probably see them make their move. The writings were on the wall, and I remember telling my friends back in 2010 that the UN wants to crash the world economy, manufacture scarcity and "terrorism," and then swoop in with the "solution": digital one-world currency, chip everyone, and impose Martial Law to "keep us safe." They laughed and told me I was crazy. I said we'll see.

Through the 2010s, life happened, and I stopped researching at such a fever pitch. I met a group of friends who were more "normal" than I, and I caught myself censoring my own thoughts to fit in better. After some time, I became acclimated to my "normal" friends. They were so care-free, unburdened by a knowledge of humanity's dark corridors, and as time went on, I started to believe that maybe I had been wrong -- that perhaps I had lost my way. Maybe there wasn't a looming monolithic conspiracy that would one day come knocking on each of our doors. As 9/11, the wars in the Middle East, and the lies that caused them slipped into the background behind the noise of life, so too did my concern.

But then at the start of 2020, it happened: The grand conspiracy reared its head, came banging at our doors, and I realized I had been wrong about being wrong. If only I had trusted my intuition a decade earlier and resisted the urge to fit in, perhaps I could have sounded the trumpet. But now it was too late. They were already making their move.

The Beginning Of The End Game

When the first "cases" began to appear in Canada in March of 2020, nobody knew what was happening. The first lockdown was upon us in the blink of an eye. In the days leading up to "two weeks to flatten the curve," I had just returned from a ski resort and was feeling a bit under the weather myself. At the time, there was no data available. All we had was the word of the mainstream media, which of course was nothing but doom and gloom.

I was immediately suspicious, however. The truth is often hidden within the lie if you know how to read between the lines.

The news was trying to convince us of a deadly and dangerous new pathogen, but at the bottom of the same article, the only deaths listed were people in their 80s and 90s. When considering that the average life expectancy in Canada is around 82 years, the “very deadly and dangerous" idea didn’t seem to hold water, but there was no way of truly knowing the extent of it without any good quality data. So I closed my studio and stayed home for a few weeks. It seemed like a reasonable thing to do at the time. However, I knew better than to stay glued to the television and allow the pundits to convince me that the world was ending. As always, I wanted to see the data myself. So I watched and waited.

After seeking a test for my symptoms, I learned that Alberta (and all of Canada, as well as most of the world for that matter) was only testing people who needed immediate hospital care, due to test shortages. The nurse on the phone told me “We’re not giving out COVID tests for sore throats. If you think you need an ambulance right now, that's the only way to get tested.”

I was perplexed. The news had already reported thousands of cases and hundreds of deaths. If all of those cases and deaths were strictly people needing urgent medical care while the testing protocols ignored people like myself who only had a scratchy throat, then the fatality rate of COVID was going to be skewed and appear far more dangerous than it really was. This piqued my interest even more. But there was still no good data.

A few weeks later, the first good science emerged from Iceland. They had decided to test as much of their population as possible, whether symptomatic or not, since the population was small enough to be covered by available resources. Iceland is an Island nation, so they were the perfect sample pool for calculating a more accurate infection and case fatality rate. Sure enough, they found the prevalence of COVID to be five times higher than anticipated in the general population, and approximately *half* of total cases were *completely asymptomatic* (or in other words, *not sick at all*). Another 48% had mild flu-like symptoms, leaving only 2% of cases requiring medical treatment, and only a fraction of those cases (<1%) died. They also noted that the worst cases and deaths were heavily weighted towards the elderly and already ill. More than 98% of cases required no medical treatment and would recover just fine on their own. The risk of death or serious complications for healthy people below the age of 60 was almost nonexistent, and they still hadn't tested everyone, which meant these numbers were most likely still inflated.

This was fantastic news! So there it was. The science had been followed and the truth was clear for all to see. If a layman like me could figure all of this out, then surely the highly trained health authorities knew, too. Case closed, right?

Well, apparently not.

Despite the data getting better from this point, showing increasingly that COVID is not a threat to the average person, the fear-mongering continued to ramp up. Health officials ignored the good news: natural immunity, recovery rates, and age stratification. Cheap and effective cures were demonized without even being given a chance. Two weeks came and went but the lockdowns stayed. Then came the masks. Then came the fact-checkers. "Follow the science," they said, while refusing to take their own advice.

But the scariest part was watching my peers fall for the lies. It was 9/11 all over again. The reality was available for anyone who cared to look, yet the mainstream media had become the arbiter of truth, singing an entirely different tune, convincing us that we were not smart enough to interpret what our eyes were showing us. When my friends began repeating the ridiculous narratives back to me, looking at me funny, and speaking to me differently when I tried to explain the hard data which proved otherwise, I knew we were in trouble.

The more I dug, the clearer it became that the government was not interested in facts and was instead pushing an agenda.

It was all about a new vaccine right from the beginning.

In all of the scientific history of masks, they had never been effective in controlled trials. They had shown consistently to cause hypoxia and no benefit or even worse outcomes for infections. Suddenly in March of 2020, masks were deemed effective when a handful of very unscientific studies (including a “study" on *hamsters*) showed up and claimed otherwise, and of course the media ignored the entire hundred year history of masks in favor of the latter.

Fear and division were being overtly encouraged, and I could see exactly where all of this was going.

My “normal” friends told me I was overreacting. That I was too deep down the rabbit hole. That nobody would ever get a ticket for not wearing a mask, and that the lockdowns would be over in a few weeks. A year and a half later, these same friends are now vaccinated and won't talk to me.

Conformity: A More Dangerous Contagion

Governments are the most dangerous thing on Earth, far more dangerous than any virus. Not even the Spanish Flu can hold a candle to the hundreds of millions of people who have been slaughtered by their own ruling class.

Democide is a concept proposed by U.S. political scientist Rudolph Rummel to describe "the intentional killing of an unarmed or disarmed person by government agents acting in their authoritative capacity and pursuant to government policy or high command." This term includes acts not directly covered by "genocide," such as criminal omission and neglect, or forced labor camps. According to Rummel, democide surpassed war as the leading cause of non-natural death in the 20th century. Statistically, you are more likely to be killed by an agent of your own government than by any other human. But clearly history does not light the way, as so many cheer and clamor to give the government more power over them, not realizing that compliance and conformity are two necessary requirements for democide.

In many ways, our government has already launched an assault against the people of this nation. The national media, and even the Prime Minister himself, are already demonizing anyone who doesn't want a vaccine that nobody needs. The vaccine mandates have arrived just as swiftly as the concept was dismissed as a "dangerous conspiracy theory" that would never come to pass only six months ago. Now my fellow citizens are repeating the rhetoric and cheering for the scenario they said would never happen. There are real people out there who are convinced I should be made a second class citizen for not wanting a gene therapy with less than six months of safety data, and which admittedly doesn't prevent infection or transmission. None of this bodes well.

So, how did we stray so far into the lie when the truth has been so clear from the beginning? Ah yes, that's right; the almighty "consensus." We have the "experts" to thank for our slide down the slippery slope from "just wear a mask when you shop" to "get vaccinated or you can't shop, period."

I've spoken to many proponents of government interventions, and a common thread runs through all of them. Since there is no good data to support any of these soul-crushing countermeasures, if I get them to talk to me long enough, without fail, they get cornered by the data, and always fall back on the same argument: "Well, if these measures didn't work, we wouldn't be doing them. The scientists would have figured it out by now." They don't know how or why it works. The only thing they know is that the experts say it does. The "consensus" itself is cited as if it were evidence.

But do the experts really know better? It's not like they speak a different language. Why is "the science" only alluded to, and never described? Most of the relevant data breaks down to simple grade school math, and can be understood by anyone, yet it's been a year and a half without an audit and the charade continues unchecked.

Crossing The Line

The COVID-19 era has brought an old saying to the front of my mind;

"If everyone else jumped off a bridge,
would you do it too?"

My mother used to ask me this question whenever I would justify my actions with the logic that: "my friends did it." My mother asked me this for good reason. She was trying to teach me how to think for myself. She knew that the group could have a strong effect on perception. A consensus can often bypass individual scrutiny. When we see the majority of others behaving in a synchronous way, we assume that their behavior is correct, and we want to fit in. But just because everyone is doing it doesn't make it right.

When we appeal to authority, or to the "wisdom of the group", this opens the door to all sorts of horrors. Many of us have heard of the Stanford and Milgram experiments (worth looking into if you haven't) but there was a lesser known series of fascinating studies conducted between 1950 and 1965 by Dr. Solomon Asch, an American psychologist. He was interested in group consensus, and the power a group can have on an individual. I think his findings are very applicable today.

Asch placed a naive participant (the "target") in a room with seven actors and told them they were taking an eye exam. The group was presented with a graphic showing three lines of different lengths, and a fourth line which was the same length as one of the other three. The group was asked to identify which line was the same length as the example, and had to announce their answer aloud, one by one, with the target individual placed near the end of the line. The actors were instructed to provide pre-planned responses, and the target didn't know everyone else was in on it. Asch wanted to see if the target could be persuaded to make a clearly incorrect choice due to group pressure.

The results showed a strong correlation. The actors unanimously provided the correct answer for the first two trials, and unanimously provided a wrong answer in the third. In all of the trials where the correct answer was provided, the target always provided the correct answer. But out of 12 critical trials where the group provided the wrong answer, 75% of participants conformed at least once, and on average about one third of total answers conformed to the incorrect consensus.

The subsequent interviews were just as interesting as the experiment itself. The biggest conformers were also the least aware, exhibiting what Asch called a "distortion of perception." Those who agreed with the consensus in 50% or more of the trials truly believed that the group was correct and were apparently totally unaware that wrong answers were being given. These participants had allowed the group to think for them entirely. These, however, were a small minority of the conformists. The majority of conformists instead expressed a "distortion of judgement." They explained that as the group answered differently over time, they concluded they must be interpreting the data incorrectly, and the group must know something they did not. After a period of giving the right answer, they began to conform with the group. They were aware of the discord between themselves and the group, but the pressure was enough to make them doubt themselves to the point of providing a wrong answer. The rest of the participants exhibited a "distortion of action." They claimed to know what the correct answer was but went with the consensus to avoid the discomfort of being the odd one out. All of the conformists and all of their reasons had one thing in common: a lack of self-confidence. They had all, to some degree, placed their trust with the group instead of their own discernment. Even the ones who suspected, or outright knew, that the group was wrong were not brave enough to stand up for themselves and challenge the status quo. The problem was not the ability to discern, but the courage to stand alone.

On the other hand, those who consistently resisted the group pressure felt no different than the conformists. They too expressed that at times they had doubted themselves, or that they had considered "going along to get along" so as not to feel extricated from the group. They persevered with what they thought was the right answer, however, because that's what they had been asked to do. The main differing factor for these people who did not yield was the willingness to go against the grain rather than just the ability to judge. They trusted themselves and wanted to do what they saw as the right thing rather than the popular thing. While most participants were able to judge the data correctly, the main difference in outcome was bravery.

Dr. Asch demonstrated the power of groupthink and how easily the individual can slip into conformity, but by conducting variations of his original experiment he made further important discoveries about the nature of conformity.

The motivating factor seemed to be the unanimity of the group rather than the overall size. He found, for example, that the size of the group mattered, but only up to a point. It is not so difficult to disagree with one other person. With one other person, conformity was only 3%. With two, it rose to 13%. Three or more brought it up to 32% (1/3rd) but adding more had no further effect. In one variation, the target wrote down their answer. Conformity significantly decreased when the target responses were written and therefore exempt from the scrutiny of the group. When the difficulty of the task increased (i.e. the difference in length of the bars becomes less obvious) conformity increased, showing that when we are uncertain, we look to others for confirmation. Conformity increased when the group was perceived to be an authority or more knowledgeable on the subject. We can infer much from all of this, but most important was the revelation of a "True Partner." By adding only one "friendly" actor who gave the correct answer while the rest of the group still answered wrong, conformity dropped to 5%. When the friendly actor was removed, conformity shot up again. The size of the group didn't matter. All it took was one other person to break up the unanimity of the group, and that was enough to give others the confidence to speak their true thoughts. It turns out that people can snap out of conformity just as quickly as they slipped into it, with a little help from a friend.

Further studies conducted by researchers in the 70s and 80s challenged Asch's original findings. Perrin and Spencer et al. ran an exact replica of Asch's 1950s study but were unable to replicate the same level of conformity. In fact, out of 396 trials, only once did the target comply with the erroneous majority. They dubbed Asch's experiment a "child of its time," proposing that the climate in the 1950s was much different and more conducive to conformity than the 70s and 80s. The newer study was performed specifically on mathematics, science, and engineering students, however, who were naturally more inclined towards trusting their own analysis. But besides the difference in sample pool, in many ways Perrin and Spencer were correct. The 70s and 80s when their experiments were conducted were a much different time. Freedom of expression, free speech, and individuality were at the forefront of the American collective. In contrast, during the post war backdrop of Asch's experiments, America was deeply entrenched in an anti-communist stance, socialist sympathies were demonized, and adherence to American nationalism was strongly encouraged.

But human evolution does not follow a linear path. We often progress and regress through the same cycles of behavior many times throughout generations. If Asch's study, and the tendency to conformity itself, could be a child of its time, then so could Perrin and Spencer's non-conformist results.

The innate drive for a human being to belong to a group and to be accepted by others is ever present. The fact should be obvious to anyone because it is our nature, and it is an aspect of our nature which can be exploited at any time. So, how would the average person score now? It has been yet another 40 years since those findings by Perrin and Spencer. What would happen if Asch's experiments were conducted again today?

Well, I propose that there is no need to wonder. Look around. Asch's experiment is being conducted all around us. North American society and much of the “civilized” world has shifted to a place where the group is revered and individuality shunned. Society has once again leaned into the prime tenet of a groupthink model, but our current state of technology pushes the potentials of the Asch effect to an extreme. Modern society is like Asch's experiment supercharged and on steroids.

Asch's experiments taught us that when an opinion is subject to scrutiny, it is more likely to align with the group scrutinizing.

The prevalence of social media has connected everyone, but instead of liberating us from our isolation, it has sent us further into it, unable to speak freely or risk being canceled by the mob. Our connectedness ensures that our views are made as public as possible.

Asch's experiments taught us that individuals seek and over trust authority, especially when the correct answers are unclear.

The government and media overwhelm us with conflicting and changing messaging, moving goalposts, dishonest/obscured data, and present hand-picked "experts" who all sing in chorus to tell us how to make sense of it all.

Asch's experiments taught us that it is not the size of the group, but the unanimity of the group that is so persuasive.

Dissenting voices are censored, ridiculed, and reprimanded as publicly as possible to smooth out the "consensus" and discourage anyone else from stepping out of rank.

Asch's experiments taught us that one other person speaking truth to a lie encourages others to do the same. But in Asch's experiment, the "friendly actor" was still allowed to speak freely. What happens when a friendly actor speaks out, but they are ridiculed, shamed, and "fact checked" for the effort? These are indeed unprecedented times. Dr. Asch would be horrified.

Challenging the consensus is uncomfortable, no matter how unreasonable the consensus is. In the last year, how many people have you heard explain away their behavior with something akin to; "Yeah it's dumb but I'm just going along to get along." The problem with that excuse can be summed up eloquently by Asch himself.

> *"The tendency to conformity in our society is so strong that reasonably intelligent and well-meaning young people are willing to call white black. This is a matter of concern. It raises questions about our ways of education and about the values that guide our conduct."*

When truth is no longer an objective value which guides our conduct, not worthy of individual scrutiny, but merely a matter of whatever the consensus is, we are in trouble. This allows others to think for us. When the consensus changes, we change right along with it, without thinking twice. The COVID narrative has already shifted drastically multiple times on the topics of risk to the public, masks, natural immunity, lab leak theory, vaccine efficacy and safety, vaccine passports and more, and nobody even bats and eye. Yesterday's conspiracy theories and fact-checks are today's reality, and it seems as if most people don't notice, or care. But is that true? Or are the majority of people suspicious but just "going along to get along" due to massive group pressure?

We are up against a monolith that would make Dr. Solomon Asch blush, but we can still learn much from his experiments. The power of one voice speaking truth to a lie is worth many more who are on the fence. If our society really is a giant Asch experiment, then the saving grace is that the majority of conforming participants knew or suspected they knew what the right answer was, but they were just too scared to go against the perceived consensus. But it only took *one other voice of reason* to give them the courage to join the ranks of objective truth.

We have an additional hurdle, though. Since the relevant information is so heavily suppressed, it is up to us to provide it. We must be brave enough to push through the wall of censorship and stand up to the slander. We need to show people what the truth is as well as endorse it.

Censorship is so rampant because it only takes a small number to break up the unanimity. Conformity may be contagious, but so is bravery, and bravery is exponentially more powerful. That is why I do what I do. I swim upstream in the hopes that I can inspire others to do the same, and I encourage you to join me. Be brave my friends: Resist the currents of conformity. Analyze and decide for yourself and speak the truth in whatever capacity is available to you. That is the most important contribution anyone can make. When we stand on our own, we challenge the ineffable consensus, and eventually, when enough of us fly our flag over the landscape, the spell will be broken. The majority of people are able to discern the truth when properly shown and encouraged. It is the bravery to go against the grain that makes all the difference in letting the truth come to light. I know you are out there, and there are many more of us than you think. Join us. Be brave, my friends. Let's end the experiment.

Bringing It Home

For those who want homework, I believe I've found the best formula for dismantling the narrative. There are so many avenues to the conversation from virus isolation to the lab leak theory, and it is easy to get lost in the reeds. It is important to be as educated as possible, but when educating the uninitiated, it is more important to be clear, concise, rock solid, and relevant. It needs to be as easy to digest and irrefutable as possible, so with that in mind I think the scam can be best summed up with the following;

Total all-cause mortality, total ICU admissions, age stratification of deaths, testing protocols, definition of "covid case" and "covid death," Laos, Vietnam, Thailand, China, and Nigeria.

Let's break it down from the top;

The Numbers: Total All-Cause Mortality

I'm aware of the CDC making the claim that there has been excess mortality in the US over the course of the pandemic, but there are some major problems with their data. First of all, it is not a strict year over year comparison of the total number of deaths from all causes. It is an unnecessarily complicated mathematical model based on taking a few weeks of the year and working with averages based on that time frame. This is problematic because the death rate grows slightly each year, so averaging backwards in time will always create the illusion of excess mortality. But why use a mathematical model based on a small portion of the year when you can just add up the totals? If you just do that, you see that the overall rate of death has not changed anywhere in the world during 2020. The increased rate of all-cause mortality in Canada was exactly what we would expect in any normal year, and many places, including Canada, show higher rates of death occurring during non-pandemic years in the last decade.

Even with their obvious attempt to spin what should be simple data, the amount of excess deaths being proposed by the CDC is still only around 30,000 while the official tally of "COVID deaths" is twenty times higher than that. Furthermore, even if they were shown to clearly exist, there is zero data to suggest that these excess deaths have anything to do with COVID. But even if we take their number at face value and assume it's all a direct result of a "novel virus," things *still* don't add up. If "COVID deaths" are over 600,000 in the US alone, but there are only 30,000 in excess, then what exactly are the other 570,000 "COVID deaths?" Thus, the CDC's own attempt to demonstrate "excess deaths" due to COVID inadvertently shows the exact opposite.

The Numbers: ICU

In Canada, I'm aware of two Freedom of Information requests in regard to ICU numbers that show the same phenomenon: one for Alberta, by Chris Scott, owner of The Whistle Stop Café in Mirror, AB, and another for Ontario, by Adam Skelly, former owner of Adamson BBQ in Etobicoke. But hey, if you want to join the ranks of the Brave, you can always file your own. They will all show the same thing as Alberta and Ontario: nothing changed. Previous "non-pandemic" years (2017/18) racked up *more ICU admissions* than the full-blown "pandemic" in 2020. Go figure. This statistic alone destroys the narrative full stop and watching people's reactions to this information is always very interesting. The most common response is, "This can't be true. I don't trust it. It's just a chart." But it is true, and the data comes straight from the government. The ICU data falls directly in line with and corroborates the all-cause mortality data. Despite the hysteria about a novel virus, nothing has changed in 2020.

The Numbers: COVID Mortality and Age Stratification

Next, I cannot stress enough how important it is to bring the age stratification of deaths to the forefront of our collective wisdom. The media is now trying to convince us that it's a good idea to vaccinate all the children, but a simple glance at the official government numbers unequivocally shows otherwise. As of August 27, 2021, in all of Canada, since the start of the "pandemic," we have had 16 deaths in people aged 19 or younger. *Sixteen.* And keep in mind that this is a year and a half worth of data. To help put this in perspective, the same age group for the calendar year 2018-2019 suffered:

48 deaths from *influenza/pneumonia*

55 deaths from diseases of the heart

346 deaths from malignant neoplasms (cancers)

481 deaths from intentional self-harm and suicides

652 deaths from *unintentional accidents.*

So why isn't the government launching any campaigns about heart health, mental health and emotional support, childhood cancer or influenza, or vehicle safety, considering that these problems all range from 200% to 3975% more "deadly" to our children than COVID. Just a hunch, but I'd bet it has something to do with the fact that there is no vaccine manufactured for profit by a private company that can "protect" children from unintentional accidents.

Beyond the 16 deaths under the age of 19, as of August 27, 2021, in Canada, according to official government data, we have:

20-29 years: 68 deaths

30-39 years: 152 deaths

40-49 years: 349 deaths

Let's pause for a moment to acknowledge that over a year and a half, in a nation of almost 40 million, we have a total of *585 COVID deaths below the age of 50.* To help put that in perspective, for the calendar year 2018-2019, Canada had 16,174 cancer deaths below the age of 50. You can't tell me the government is looking out for us while they completely ignore something that causes 2664% more deaths than COVID.

50-59 years: 1020 deaths

60-69 years: 2606 deaths

70-79 years: 5435 deaths

80+ years: 17,109 deaths

By using official government statistics at face value and grade school math, we don't need the help of any so-called experts to make an incredible revelation. The overwhelming majority of deaths in Canada (63%) are at the age of general life expectancy, and the deaths drop off sharply from there. Eighty-four percent of all COVID deaths in Canada are *over the age of 70,* and 94% of the deaths are over the age of 60. Deaths below the age of 60 only constitute around 6% of COVID deaths. Once again, it is not possible to call these figures a "pandemic." But what is a "COVID death" anyway? This brings me to the next point.

Classification and Testing

Remember my experience trying to get tested at the start of 2020? Well, shortly thereafter, things took a sharp turn in the other direction, and the protocols became so loose that pretty much anything could be considered a "COVID death." According to the official WHO guidelines, all that is needed for classification of death "due to" COVID is a positive, or even "presumed positive" test result. Essentially, the only criteria needed to diagnose a death as due to COVID is "a positive PCR test at or around the time of death." That's it. It doesn't matter if the person had three comorbidities and was given a week to live, if that test comes back positive, that's a COVID death. Dr. Ngozi Ezike, Director of Public Health in Illinois, spilled the beans herself during a press conference last year, saying that "the case definition of COVID death is very simplistic... even if they died of a clear alternate cause, but the test was positive, that would still be considered a COVID death."

So, what about the testing, then? If all of the numbers hinge so heavily on the test, we'd better be sure it's accurate. Enter the PCR test. PCR stands for polymerase chain reaction and is a process of amplification. It takes a sample of something so small that it cannot be seen with a microscope and magnifies it exponentially until it can be measured. The problem with this is that with enough magnification, it can find viral particles still kicking around from a flu infection you had when you were eight years old. If we use too many cycles of amplification and use viral particles alone to determine a "case," this is a recipe for many false positives, especially as more and more of the general population comes into contact with the virus. In Episode 641 of the "This Week in Virology" podcast, which aired on July 16, 2020, Anthony Fauci himself said that anything over 35 cycles is unusable, and is just "dead nucleotides, period." To quote him directly (parenthesis added for context):

> *"...If you get [perform the PCR test at] a cycle threshold of 35 or more...the chances of it being replication-confident [aka accurate] are miniscule... you almost never can culture virus [detect a true positive result] from a 37 threshold cycle...even 36..."*

His comments are around the 4:00 minute mark of the podcast for anyone who wants to look it up. Meanwhile, the FDA's official guidelines recommend *40 cycles,* and all across Canada, Europe, the US, and the world at large, hospitals are using PCR tests with cycles anywhere from 36-50. The inventor of the PCR test himself, Kary Mullis, has stated in no unclear terms that the PCR test should not be used the way we are using it. He explained that it is "too good" at finding particles that are likely irrelevant and should never be used in the absence of other diagnostic measures. It should be part of an array and not the only diagnostic tool. Yet this is exactly what we are doing.

An interesting side note is that hospitals in the US are being paid to classify patients and deaths as COVID. Look up Dr. Scott Jensen for more details on this topic. Hospitals were being offered up to *$40,000 per COVID death.* It doesn't take a genius to figure this out. It's exactly what it looks like. Loose definitions and monetary incentives to abuse them. This is the crux of the whole scam, as it has turned into a PCR driven "casedemic." If the cycles were reduced, or even better yet, we only counted people who were clinically ill, the "pandemic" would vanish overnight.

Anomalous Regions

Finally, all of the regions I mentioned are of particular interest because they are anomalies when it comes to COVID statistics, including, of all places, China. Johns Hopkins has put out an official real-time COVID world map, and if you know where to look, you will find statistics that are impossible to justify. Search the map, and even Google for any of the mentioned regions, and be amazed. These are some of the most populous countries in the world, some of which never bothered much with countermeasures, including vaccinations, yet they all have less total deaths than the province of Ontario. Some have less than half.

For the birthplace of the virus, China has done remarkably well overall with only 4636 total deaths as of August 2021. Shanghai has a population half the size of Canada jammed into one city, and to date it has *seven* COVID deaths. There have been essentially no COVID deaths in China since March of 2020. It's almost as if China's only goal was to set the stage for the rest of the world, and then they stopped the farce as soon as their program was adopted everywhere else. This statistic is so strange that as of August 2021, Google will not even graph the deaths in China. The option is greyed out. It will only show the cases on a graph, but even the cases abruptly trickle down to nothing in March of 2020. How is it possible that the entire country of China, where the virus originated, with a population of 1.44 *billion*, has less than one fifth of the deaths of Canada? To further put this into perspective, Canada has a population that is 2.7% as large as China, yet Canada has 479% more deaths. Does that make any sense at all?

Thailand and Vietnam both have *very* interesting charts. If you simply look up "Thailand/Vietnam COVID deaths" on Google, you will see what I mean. Thailand, with its population of 70 million, had managed to keep COVID deaths below 50 without vaccinations until April of 2021. One more time for those in the back: *<50 deaths in a population of 70 million over a year and a half. No vaccine.* Thailand began their vaccine rollout slowly with healthcare workers at the start of March. Then suddenly, after a year and half of no deaths, for the first time ever, deaths began to creep up in April of 2021. Thailand began their mass vaccination rollout very recently, in mid-July, and since then the deaths have gone through the roof. In a matter of months, Thailand went from less than 50 deaths to 12,103, and *6732 of those occurred in* ***August 2021 alone.*** Vietnam tells an almost identical tale. The chart shows nobody dying until the deaths suddenly began to spike in June/July of 2021. Vietnam now has 12,138 deaths, and *10,067 of those are from* ***August of 2021.*** Vietnam began their mass vaccine rollout In June. They went from 4% with one dose to just under 20% with one dose from mid-July until August 2021, and that happens to be exactly when the deaths skyrocketed for the first time ever. If anyone ever tries to tell you that vaccines are safe, effective, and the only way out of this, show them this data.

Laos appears to have simply refused to play ball after the first few weeks, with a population of 7.3 million, a shared border with China, and *fourteen deaths* as of August 2021.

Nigeria, on the other hand, has less COVID deaths than the state of Iowa. Iowa has a population of 3.1 million. Nigeria has a population of 201 million and never cared much for non-medical interventions (lockdown, masks etc.). So, how is it remotely possible that Iowa has approximately twice as many deaths as Nigeria? This is not possible based on the narrative we've been fed: that COVID is everywhere and is very dangerous. But the reality should be clear by now. There are different rubrics at play, and ultimately COVID is a game of *reclassification* and nothing more. The nations with low death counts are employing much stricter definitions, which include using PCR tests in proper context and at a reasonable cycle threshold, while nations with runaway death counts are simply using high threshold PCR tests and extremely loose definitions of "COVID death" to classify as many otherwise normal deaths as they can as "COVID deaths." This reality is irrefutably demonstrated by these key talking points. We can go back and forth about whether or not the virus has been isolated all day, and that is indeed an important angle in getting to the bottom of this, but why rest on such a technical discussion when it is not even necessary to expose the scam? The truth has been right in front of our eyes the whole time according to "official" statistics, statements, and guidelines. You just need to be brave enough to look for it, uncover it, and be braver yet to speak it.

The Truth Doesn't Care, But You Should

This has been a brief summary of my awakening to the world, a detailed account of my awakening to the COVID scam, plenty of food for thought, and a plethora of ammunition for the fight ahead. As you can probably tell by now, I let logic and reason dictate my beliefs and opinions. Nothing more, and nothing less. The truth is always there, no matter how well hidden. It can never be destroyed, only obscured. It remains patiently, ever present, and ready to be discovered by someone brave enough to see it for what it is rather than what they have been told it is. If we allow others to dictate our thoughts, we betray our own powers of observation and discernment, and may end up calling white, black without even realizing it. After discovering that the wool had been pulled over my eyes this way, I vowed to never let that happen again, and I have been paying acute attention to the world I inhabit ever since.

What people perceive as my Bravery is really just a deep understanding. How could I possibly act any other way knowing all that I have disclosed here? I could not idly stand by knowing what I know. The implications are far too strong. Therefore my bravery is a natural by-product of my understanding. In Asch's experiments, it was those who were most sure of themselves who stood up to the consensus. They had the deepest *understanding* of the data presented to them. But the trick of Asch's experiments was that the lines were just similar enough to sow doubt when confronted with the pressure of the group. In a similar way, I believe there is an inner conflict happening within most people. They know that something feels "off," but the data being presented along with the consensus about it is just convincing enough to keep them doubting their instincts. But there is no arguing with the data I have presented here. That's why it is never spoken of, and that is why we must show it to them. What if Asch's experiment had made the answer overwhelmingly obvious? Would anyone have fallen for it? Perhaps we should try this variation ourselves.

To all of the awakened souls, whether you've been awake longer than me or you just woke up right now, you are awake because you trust your own understanding and do not let anyone else think for you. And now, we must teach others to do the same – we must make the truth overwhelmingly obvious, and shatter the consensus in the process, so that even the most timid among us can step into the truth, unhindered and unafraid.

You are now equipped with all of the ingredients you need to serve up the truth as a "true partner," and blaze a trail for others to follow. Let an understanding based on logic and reason guide you, trust your judgement and instincts above all, and the secret ingredient -- Bravery -- will flow effortlessly from you.

About RC The Rapper:

Conrad Goodsir, aka "RC The Rapper" is a Canadian music producer, sound engineer, photographer, and, as the name implies, rapper. He has been an artist, audio specialist, and photographer/ videographer based in Edmonton, Alberta, Canada for the last ten years. In December of 2020, after a long hiatus, he decided to start releasing his own music again. But this time he had a purpose. After watching the totalitarian tiptoe creep into our communities, our homes, and our minds for nearly a year, RC had seen enough. He wanted to do something, and as an artist with over two decades of experience writing and recording, making music is what he does best. On Christmas Day 2020, RC released a song called "The Virus," which proposed that the real virus was fear. At the same time, he got involved in pro-freedom activism, and since then his music has been streamed hundreds of thousands of times, putting him in the spotlight for better or worse. He's received praise, support, and applause, as well as hate, condemnation, and threats. He's been slandered, censored, and fined for his efforts, and also lauded as a maverick and a hero. Needless to say, the opinions about RC are quite mixed, but he never cared much for what people say about him. In his own words, "I know who I am, and nobody can tell me otherwise. I'm someone who values the truth, pays attention to the world I live in, and acts accordingly. People say that makes me Brave, but to me that's just Logical."

RC, his music, and more can be found at
www.rctherapper.com

Be sure to check the resources section for more info and citations relating to these passages.

Thank You to the Brave Donors!

So much gratitude for all the donations that were received to help produce and publish this book! Without your support in uncertain times, this book may not have been possible.

If we ever find ourselves in situations where we want to help, we want to do something, but we just don't know how we can make a real impact, in these times you can never go wrong when you support, encourage, and believe in those who are taking action and making a difference.

When you surround yourself with the warriors of the world, the conversations become very different.

The warrior within us all is calling on us at this time to BE BRAVE, DO SOMETHING!

Thank you to these brave donors for contributing to cover the expenses to produce this book:

- Jason Christoff
- Raoul Emile
- Jonathon Hernandez
- Matt Belair
- Tina Theophanous
- Darlene Ondi
- Ted Kuntz
- Danna Bresciani
- Heidi Schimpl

About Lionheart Publishing

Lionheart Publishing was conceived by Lani, Lady Braven of the Pride, for the purpose of sharing true conscious high vibrational inspiration with divine guidance, courage, and passion. After walking away from a twenty-year career in TV/film, Lani is dedicated to sharing stories and experiences with others to help them navigate these transformational, trying, and interesting times with a brave and abundant mindset.

Whenever we speak from the heart and share stories to encourage, inspire, and empower others, we are taking courageous action in alignment with our individual guidance; we are moving into our Dharma, which is our path and our purpose for being here at this time.

This book *The Brave: Speaking Truth to Power* is the second volume in a four-part series to be completed in 2021. This book is blue to activate the throat chakra and encourage others to speak their truth and express their soul's desires and convictions.

More Books by Lionheart Publishing:

The Brave 1: Courage During Covid, is attuned to green to activate the heart chakra and the courage within us all. Published in May 2021.

The Brave 3: Elevating Human Consciousness will be indigo to attune with the Third Eye Chakra. Projected to come out in November 2021.

The Brave 4: *Manifesting 5D Earth* will be violet to attune with the Crown Chakra. Projected to come out before December 31, 2021

Lionheart Activation Journal – 30 Day Journaling Challenge to Build a Brave and Abundant Mindset, for those interested in doing their own personal growth work and developing their conversation with divine intelligence and self. Published and available.

All of these books will be available through Amazon.com and on the Lady Braven of the Pride Website at
www.LadyBravenofthePride.com under
Lionheart Publishing.